Assessing Native and Introduced Fish Predation on Migrating Juvenile Salmon in Priest Rapids and Wanapum Reservoirs, Columbia River, Washington, 2009–11

By Timothy D. Counihan and Jill M. Hardiman, U.S. Geological Survey; Dave S. Burgess and Katrina E. Simmons, Washington Department of Fish and Wildlife; Glen S. Holmberg, U.S. Geological Survey; and Josh A. Rogala and Rochelle R. Polacek, Washington Department of Fish and Wildlife

Prepared in cooperation with the Washington Department of Fish and Wildlife

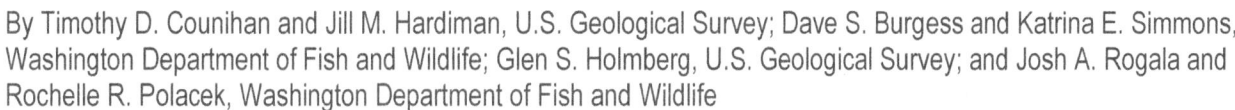

Open-File Report 2012–1130

U.S. Department of the Interior
U.S. Geological Survey

U.S. Department of the Interior
KEN SALAZAR, Secretary

U.S. Geological Survey
Marcia K. McNutt, Director

U.S. Geological Survey, Reston, Virginia: 2012

For more information on the USGS—the Federal source for science about the Earth, its natural and living resources, natural hazards, and the environment, visit *http://www.usgs.gov* or call 1-888-ASK-USGS.

For an overview of USGS information products, including maps, imagery, and publications, visit *http://www.usgs.gov/pubprod*

To order this and other USGS information products, visit *http://store.usgs.gov*

Contents

Figures

iv

Tables

Conversion Factors and Abbreviations and Acronyms

Conversion Factors

Inch/Pound to SI

Multiply	By	To obtain
Length		
inch (in.)	2.54	centimeter (cm)
inch (in.)	25.4	millimeter (mm)
foot (ft)	0.3048	meter (m)
mile (mi)	1.609	kilometer (km)
Area		
acre	0.4047	hectare (ha)
acre	0.004047	square kilometer (km^2)
Flow rate		
cubic foot per second (ft^3/s)	0.02832	cubic meter per second (m^3/s)
Mass		
ounce, avoirdupois (oz)	28.35	gram (g)

I to Inch/Pound

Multiply	By	To obtain
Length		
centimeter (cm)	0.3937	inch (in.)
millimeter (mm)	0.03937	inch (in.)
meter (m)	3.281	foot (ft)
kilometer (km)	0.62137	mile (mi)
Area		
hectare (ha)	0.003861	square mile (mi^2)
hectare (ha)	2.47105	acre
Flow rate		
cubic meter per second (m^3/s)	35.31	cubic foot per second (ft^3/s)
Mass		
gram (g)	0.03527	ounce, avoirdupois (oz)

Temperature in degrees Celsius (°C) may be converted to degrees Fahrenheit (°F) as follows: °F=(1.8×°C)+32

Abbreviations and Acronyms

Abbreviation or Acronym	Definition
BiOp	Biological Opinion
BRZ	Boat Restricted Zone
CPUE	Catch per unit effort
EPA	U.S. Environmental Protection Agency
EMAP	Environmental Monitoring and Assessment Program
FERC	Federal Energy Regulatory Commission
GIS	Geographic information system
GPP	Generator Powered Pulsator
GPS	Global Positioning System
Grant PUD	Public Utility District No. 2 of Grant County, Washington
n	number
PRCC	Priest Rapids Coordinating Committee
PRP	Priest Rapids Project
RM	River mile
SE	Standard error
SOP	Standard Operating Procedures
spp	species
USGS	U.S. Geological Survey
WDFW	Washington Department of Fish and Wildlife

Assessing Native and Introduced Fish Predation on Migrating Juvenile Salmon in Priest Rapids and Wanapum Reservoirs, Columbia River, Washington, 2009–11

By Timothy D. Counihan[1], Jill M. Hardiman[1], Dave S. Burgess[2], Katrina E. Simmons[2], Glen S. Holmberg[1], Josh A. Rogala[2], and Rochelle R. Polacek[2]

Abstract

Hydroelectric development on the mainstem Columbia River has created a series of impoundments that promote the production of native and non-native piscivores. Reducing the effects of fish predation on migrating juvenile salmonids has been a major component of mitigating the effects of hydroelectric development in the Columbia River basin. Extensive research examining juvenile salmon predation has been conducted in the lower Columbia River. Fewer studies of predation have been done in the Columbia River upstream of its confluence with the Snake River; the most comprehensive predation study being from the early 1990s. The Public Utility District No. 2 of Grant County, Washington initiated a northern pikeminnow removal program in 1995 in an attempt to reduce predation on juvenile salmonids. However, there has been no assessment of the relative predation within the Priest Rapids Project since the removal program began. Further, there is concern about the effects of piscivores other than northern pikeminnow (*Ptychocheilus oregonensis*), such as channel catfish (*Ictalurus punctatus*), smallmouth bass (*Micropterus dolomieu*), and walleye (*Sander vitreus*, formerly *Stizostedion vitreum*). The Public Utility District No. 2 of Grant County, Washington and the Priest Rapids Coordinating Committee requested that the U.S. Geological Survey, in collaboration with the Washington Department of Fish and Wildlife, assist them in evaluating the effects of native and introduced predatory fish on migrating juvenile salmon. From 2009 to 2010, we conducted sampling in the 103 kilometers (64 river miles) of the Columbia River from the tailrace of Rock Island Dam downstream to the tailrace of Priest Rapids Dam. To assess predation, we used electrofishing to collect northern pikeminnow, smallmouth bass, and walleye to analyze their diets during 2009 and 2010. In 2009, we used methods to allow comparisons to a previous study conducted in 1993. During 2009, we also used an alternate sampling strategy using habitat data and geographic information system software to select sites and allocate samples. In 2010, we used the data collected during 2009 to further refine our sampling design, with the intent of using the data collected during 2010 to formulate a design strategy for implementation during 2011. Based on the results of 2011, we would then propose a strategy for future studies. However, during 2011, our efforts were redirected to specifically address factors that may be affecting steelhead trout survival in the Priest Rapids Reservoir, Columbia River.

---

[1] U.S. Geological Survey
[2] Washington Department of Fish and Wildlife

We used the catch and diet data collected in 2009 and 2010 to estimate relative abundance, consumption, and predation indices for northern pikeminnow and smallmouth bass. Despite extensive sampling in the study area in 2009 and 2010, very few channel catfish and walleye were captured. The mean total lengths of northern pikeminnow were much lower than those observed in 1993; suggesting that efforts to remove northern pikeminnow in the study area may be shifting the population towards smaller fish. The northern pikeminnow predation index values were lower in 2009 than in the 1993 study. The reduced predation levels observed may be due to the prevalence of smaller pikeminnow in our catches than in catches reported in 1993. Predation by smallmouth bass was lower in 2009 than in 2010, and generally was greater than predation for northern pikeminnow. Predation for northern pikeminnow was concentrated in the tailrace areas of Priest Rapids, Wanapum, and Rock Island Dams; predation for smallmouth bass was concentrated in the forebay and mid-reservoir sections of the study area. Our results indicate areas where control measures for smallmouth bass could be concentrated to reduce predation in the Priest Rapids Project.

Introduction

Hydroelectric development in the Columbia River basin has transformed the Columbia River from a high-gradient riverine system to a series of impoundments created by hydroelectric dams. Anadromous juvenile salmonids migrating through the Columbia River experience a variety of hazards that affect their survival as they migrate from freshwater rearing habitats to the ocean. Direct effects associated with dam passage (for example, instantaneous mortality, injury, and loss of equilibrium) and indirect effects (such as predation, disease, and physiological stress) contribute to the total mortality of seaward-migrating salmonids. Many studies (Raymond, 1979; Stier and Kynard, 1986; Iwamato and others, 1994; Muir and others, 1995; Bickford and Skalski, 2000; Timko and others, 2007a, 2007b) have been conducted to estimate dam, reach, and route-specific (that is through spillways, bypass areas, and turbines) survival of juvenile salmon to help identify the potential sources of mortality. Based on these studies and the endangered or threatened status of anadromous salmonid stocks in the Columbia River basin, management actions are being implemented to improve survival of juvenile salmonid migrants. In some instances, management strategies are in response to stipulated criteria as part of Federal Energy Regulatory Commission (FERC) hydroelectric project relicensing agreements. For instance, as part of the FERC license issued to the Public Utility District No. 2 of Grant County, Washington (Grant PUD) for the operation of the Priest Rapids Project on April 17, 2008 (Federal Energy Regulatory Commission, 2008), performance standards (passage survival rates) were established for Grant PUD in the National Marine Fisheries Service 2004 Biological Opinion (National Marine Fisheries Service, 2004), as adapted in the "Terms and Conditions" of the 2008 Biological Opinion (National Marine Fisheries Service, 2008). The 2006 Priest Rapids Project Salmon and Steelhead Settlement Agreement (U.S. Fish and Wildlife Service and others, 2006) requires that the same survival standards be met for salmonid species not listed under the Endangered Species Act.

Grant PUD is working to improve juvenile salmonid survival through their hydroelectric developments and the river environment affected by the construction and operation of these structures, collectively referred to as the Priest Rapids Project (PRP). Management actions to improve survival include altering dam operations, modifying the physical structure of hydroelectric projects, and reducing predator effects. For instance, surface flow alternatives to promote egress through the near-dam environment have resulted in improved passage at Priest Rapids and Wanapum Dams, where surface bypass systems are in operation; a prototype top-spill bypass was installed at Priest Rapids Dam in 2006 (Harmon and Parks, 1980; Ransom and Steig, 1995; Coutant and Whitney, 2000; Johnson and others, 2005; Robichaud and others, 2005; Timko and others, 2007a, 2007b). In 2008, modifications to the operation of the prototype top-spill included additional bottom and sluiceway spill at adjacent gates, which increased passage effectiveness and warranted further testing (Sullivan and others, 2001). These alterations have resulted in some improvements in fish collection efficiency and survival.

Predation in the Columbia River is a significant factor affecting survival of downstream migrating salmonids (Beamesderfer and Rieman, 1991; Burley and Poe, 1994; Ward and others, 1995; Petersen and Ward, 1999; Petersen, 2002). Beamesderfer and others (1996) estimated that about 16.4 million out-migrating juvenile anadromous salmonids were consumed annually by northern pikeminnow (*Ptychocheilus oregonensis*) in the Columbia and Snake Rivers prior to the Northern Pikeminnow Management Program for the lower Columbia and Snake Rivers and Northern Pikeminnow Removal Programs implemented collectively by Grant PUD, Public Utility District No. 1 of Chelan County, Washington, and Public Utility District No. 1 of Douglas County, Washington. When compared to the estimated 200 million juvenile anadromous salmonids produced in the combined Columbia–Snake River systems, northern pikeminnow are believed to consume approximately 8 percent of all downstream migrants, although 6.5 percent are believed to be consumed downstream of The Dalles Dam (Beamesderfer and others, 1996).

Extensive research on juvenile salmon predation has been conducted in the Columbia River downstream of its confluence with the Snake River. Fewer studies of predation on juvenile salmonids have been done in the Columbia River upstream of its confluence with the Snake River, the most comprehensive study was from the early 1990s (Burley and Poe, 1994). The Grant PUD initiated a northern pikeminnow removal program in 1995 in an attempt to reduce predation on juvenile salmonids (Garner and Keeler, 2008, 2009). However, no assessment has been made of the relative predation within the PRP since the removal program began. Furthermore, there is concern about the effects of fish predators other than northern pikeminnow, such as channel catfish (*Ictalurus punctatus)*, smallmouth bass (*Micropterus dolomieu*), and walleye (*Sander vitreus*, formerly *Stizostedion vitreum*). The Grant PUD and the Priest Rapids Coordinating Committee (PRCC) requested that the U.S. Geological Survey (USGS), in collaboration with the Washington Department of Fish and Wildlife (WDFW), assist them in their efforts to evaluate the effects of native and introduced predatory fish on migrating juvenile salmon. From 2009 to 2010, we developed and conducted research to increase our understanding of predator-prey interactions within the PRP.

Our objectives in this study were to assess the current status of predation on juvenile salmonids migrating through the Priest Rapids and Wanapum Reservoirs on the Columbia River, Washington. Specifically, we were to repeat the methods of a previous study (Burley and Poe, 1994) to assess the current status of predation on juvenile salmonids from the tailrace of Rock Island Dam to the tailrace of Priest Rapids Dam on the Columbia River. In addition, we were to implement alternate study design and sampling protocols that could be used for future studies of juvenile salmonid predation within the PRP.

Study Methods

We conducted field collections of fish predators and their diets in 2009–11. In 2009, we implemented design and sampling strategies to allow comparisons to a Mid-Columbia Predation Index Study from 1993 (Burley and Poe, 1994; hereafter referred to as Burley and Poe). We replicated this study, with the exception that we sampled from the tailrace of Rock Island Dam to the tailrace of Priest Rapids Dam and modified some data collection and laboratory analysis protocols to conform to current standards and regulatory requirements. We also explored alternate sampling strategies that incorporated habitat data and geographic information system (GIS) software to select sites and allocate samples. In 2010, we continued our sampling using modified methods in our study design and sample frame design that incorporated the results from 2009. In 2011, the PRCC redirected the original study objectives to specifically assess predation effects of juvenile steelhead migrating through the Priest Rapids Development only. The results of the 2011 work are described in a separate report (Hardiman and others, 2012). We used fish collected in 2011, however, to describe certain characteristics of the predator populations (such as fish ages) and to present the results in this report.

Study Area

The PRP study area included approximately 64 river miles, from the Rock Island Dam (RM 453) tailrace to about 8 mi downstream of the Priest Rapids Dam (RM 397) in the Columbia River (fig. 1). The PRP consists of two run-of-the-river hydroelectric developments owned and operated by Grant PUD. The Priest Rapids Reservoir is about 18 mi in length, with a shoreline of 56 mi and an approximate surface area of 7,580 acres (Pfeifer and others, 2001). The Wanapum Reservoir is 38 mi in length, with 91 mi of shoreline and a surface area of 14,590 acres (Pfeifer and others, 2001). Environmental conditions during the study periods were obtained for Priest Rapids, Wanapum, and Rock Island Dams from the University of Washington's Columbia River Data Access in Real Time (DART) Web site (*http://www.cbr.washington.edu/dart/*).

Field Data Collection

Site Selection

The study area was divided into strata based on the longitudinal position of reaches in each reservoir. The construction of hydroelectric projects on the Columbia River has formed a series of impoundments that have characteristics typical of lakes and streams. The consequences of impoundment are relatively predictable; the reservoirs are more like streams immediately downstream of the upstream dam and more like lakes near the downstream dam. As such, reservoirs typically can be divided into three zones (riverine, transitional, and lacustrine), corresponding to riverine conditions (tailrace area); transition to lake conditions (mid-reservoir); and lake-like conditions near the downstream dam (forebay area). Past predation studies have shown that predation of juvenile salmonids varies longitudinally in impoundments of the Columbia River (Petersen, 1994) and that areas near hydroelectric dams, that are typically restricted to boat use (Boat Restricted Zones; BRZ), are areas where predation of juvenile salmonids is relatively high (Ward and others, 1995). The work of Petersen (1994) demonstrated that failure to account for this spatial variability resulted in bias in predation estimates. Therefore, we structured our sampling strategy, in part, based on the development of longitudinal strata in the study area.

Sampling consisted of Burley and Poe's efforts in 2009 and additional predator indexing efforts using a modified sampling design in 2009 and 2010 that incorporated the use of a GIS containing habitat features. In 2009, the longitudinal strata (that is, forebay, mid-reservoir, and tailrace) replicated the Burley and Poe (1994) study, and were approximately 3.7 mi in length with the exception of the BRZ areas (fig. 1). For the Burley and Poe efforts each of the longitudinal strata were divided into transects that were approximately 1,640 ft in length and were randomly selected for shoreline (depths of less than 10 ft) electrofishing efforts. For the predator index sampling, a GIS was used to generate a systematic grid of points spaced every 50 ft with a depth criterion of less than 10 ft within each of the longitudinal strata. Points were then randomly selected for electrofishing sites each week. Because of the smaller sizes of the BRZ areas, the entire available shoreline was sampled whenever access was provided to these areas.

Modifications to the sample design were incorporated into the 2010 sample framework, based on assessment of the 2009 sampling efforts. One constraint was the limited access to sampling in the BRZ areas because of high flows and coordination needed to cease some dam operations to safely access these areas. Therefore, we added additional strata immediately upstream of the forebay and downstream of the tailrace BRZs in 2010 (fig. 2). By adding these reaches, we were able to sample the near-BRZ areas weekly without affecting dam operations. Another sample area modification was to expand the mid-reservoir reaches in both Wanapum and Priest Rapids Reservoirs from the approximate 3.7-mi reach used in 2009 to the entire river area that was not included in one of the other sampling reaches (fig. 2). This eliminated the possibility of missing potentially important areas not sampled in 2009.

Sample Allocation

The sample allocation for the Burley and Poe efforts was designed to replicate sampling periods to capture the spring and summer periods as achieved in the 1993 study (Burley and Poe, 1994). Efforts were allocated over a 10-day sampling period for the spring and summer, where each strata would be covered twice, consisting of six randomly selected transects, with the exception of the BRZs (only two transects). To determine when to initiate sampling, because there was no rationale for mimicking the actual dates sampled in 1993, we used water temperature as a criterion to begin sampling during the spring and summer periods. Sampling for the spring was initiated when water temperatures reached approximately 12°C, and for the summer, when water temperatures were approximately 19°C. Burley and Poe's spring sampling occurred from May 27 to June 12, 2009, and summer sampling occurred from August 3 to 20, 2009.

For the 2009 and 2010 predator indexing efforts, we sampled continuously throughout the juvenile salmonid migration period, and then retrospectively determined the spring and summer periods based on Smolt Passage Indices presented on the Columbia River DART web site for Rock Island Dam. The sample design was such that the entire study area would be covered each week; and week days were randomly assigned to reaches by sample week throughout the study. Efforts allocated to the BRZ sampling were less than those allocated for the other strata because of the coordination and alteration of dam operations required to access BRZ areas. To determine the spring migration period, we summed the smolt index values for yearling Chinook, coho, and sockeye salmon, and steelhead trout, and then assumed the middle 90 percent of the run as the sampling period. In 2010, logistics prevented us from sampling until May 19, which was later than these criteria would dictate. We used the smolt passage index at Rock Island Dam for sub-yearling Chinook salmon to define the summer period so that the beginning of the summer period was the first day that the index values for Rock Island Dam exceeded and subsequently did not go below values for either yearling Chinook, coho, and sockeye salmon, and steelhead trout. In 2009, sampling occurred from May 1 to August 27, with the spring migration period defined as May 4–June 11, and the summer migration period defined as June 22–August 7. For 2010, sampling occurred from May 19 to September 3, with the spring migration period defined as May 19–June 9, and the summer period defined as June 27–August 11.

Boat Electrofishing

We used standardized operating procedures for electrofishing (available upon request) to collect predators in 2009 and 2010. Electrofishing efforts were conducted along the shoreline at preselected sites using two 18 ft-long (5.5 m-long), Smith Root® 5.0 Generator Powered Pulsator (GPP) electrofishing boats. Following the WDFW warm-water sampling protocol (Bonar and others, 2000), individual electrofishing boats were operated parallel to the shoreline at a rate of 0.6–0.9 m/h, maintained a distance from shore that allowed the inshore boom to fish entirely in the water, and avoided areas that exceeded 10 ft in depth. To facilitate fish galvanotaxis, we operated the GPP unit at approximately 1–2 amperes (amps) using a low power setting (50–500 volts) with a frequency between 30–120 Hz DC. To prevent unnecessary fish injury, we noted the behavior of fish within the electrical field and adjusted the power accordingly.

Time, personnel, and direction of travel associated with sampling also were standardized. The goal of each electrofishing boat was to electrofish each site for 600 s. The number of crew on an individual boat also was regulated to maintain a constant effort between times and boats. Each crew consisted of one boat operator and two dip netters stationed at the front of the vessel, and each crew member was outfitted with a personal flotation device. Electrofishing was always conducted downstream.

For the Burley and Poe efforts, electrofishing began 90 min before sunrise (determined using the Mattawa site from *http://www.usno.navy.mil/USNO/astronomical-applications/data-services/rs-one-year-us*) and continued until we attained a target catch of 15 northern pikeminnow from each section sampled. For the predator indexing efforts, electrofishing began no earlier than 30 min after sunset (determined using the Mattawa site from *http://www.usno.navy.mil/USNO/astronomical-applications/data-services/rs-one-year-us*) and continued until all sites were completed, weather permitting. The following information was recorded for each sample site: water temperature, specific conductance, time of day, transect start and end GPS coordinates, initials of crew, date, site designation, and power settings used to electrofish. During electrofishing, stunned fishes were placed immediately in one of the two onboard livewells equipped with a pump that continually added freshwater into the tank. After the completion of two 600-s electrofishing runs, the boat operator moored the electrofishing boat on shore where WDFW or USGS staff collected the required biological information from the captured fish. In the event that transit time between sites was extended as a result of distance or environmental conditions, crews collected the pertinent data from the captured fishes immediately after the completion of the first site.

Following standardized operating procedures (available upon request), biological information was collected for the following target species: northern pikeminnow, smallmouth and largemouth bass, channel catfish, and walleye. Because of the potential for the captured fishes to be consumed by anglers, we did not use the anesthetic commonly referred to as MS-222 per U.S. Food and Drug Administration guidelines. Therefore, all fish captured as non-lethal take were worked up in a non-anesthetized state. The collection of data from identified fish included the length, weight, and aging structures, such as scales for non-lethal-take fish and opercles for lethal-take fish. Hard structures for aging were collected from northern pikeminnow, smallmouth bass, and walleye for the duration of the fieldwork. The diets of walleye, smallmouth and largemouth bass (*Micropterus salmoides*), and walleye were collected using a lavage technique (non-lethal take), while northern pikeminnow and channel catfish (lethal take) stomachs were surgically removed. All diets were preserved (either frozen whole or contents soaked in 95-percent ethanol) and transported back to the laboratory to be analyzed for contents at a later date.

Laboratory Analyses

Aging Analysis

Scales and opercles collected in the field were transported to the Large Lakes Research Team Laboratory in Ellensburg, Washington, to be prepared for aging analysis according to standardized operating procedures (available upon request). Personnel at the WDFW aging laboratory read scales using a standard office microfiche that had the ability to alter magnifications levels. Initially, a magnification that permitted a view of the entire scale was used to examine circuli. The areas where circuli were concentrated indicated an annulus or year mark (Jearld, 1983). Each annulus from the focus or center of the scales was identified and counted to provide an estimate of a length at age for an individual fish, and data were sent to the Large Lakes Research Team Laboratory. Cleaned opercular bones were placed proximal side up in a petri dish containing 95-percent ethanol and viewed under a dissecting microscope between 60 and 120 magnification. Samples were viewed under reflected light and contrasted against a solid black background. Annuli were counted on the proximal surface in a plane from the center to the anterior opercle edge similar to Le Cren (1947). Annuli were distinguished as the band of transparent growth occurring during the slow growing season (assumed winter months) and soon after the opaque fast growth (assumed spring and summer months). Fish were assumed to have a birth date of January 1; therefore, annuli forming at the opercle edge in fall months were not counted unless there was opaque growth beyond the annuli, although for spring collections, annuli at the edge were counted (occurring after the universal birth date of January 1). Up to three readings on older, more difficult structures were made per sample until a consistent reading could be determined. The age estimation was recorded and the opercle was placed back in the sample envelope and sealed.

Mean length at age and the standard error (SE) were calculated for each age class for the three predators. Length-at-age data for northern pikeminnow, smallmouth bass, and walleye were combined for the 2009, 2010, and 2011 sampling seasons in order to increase our sample size and to reduce the amount of variation associated with aging fish. Aging data should yield a mean length-at-age trend that increases as a group of fish ages. This trend was not the case for all our predatory fish 10 years or older. Therefore, length-at-age frequencies for fish determined to be 10 years or older omitted data for fish that had a mean length of less than that of fish estimated to be 1 year younger. Decreasing confidence in age estimates for older fish when scales are used have been noted in other studies (Donabauer 2010, Erickson, 1983; Isermann and others, 2003; Hanchin, 2011).

Diet Analysis

Diet analysis was conducted in a laboratory setting using two different methodologies (SOPs available upon request), one for northern pikeminnow and another for bass and walleye. The methodology for processing northern pikeminnow stomachs involved pancreatin digestion or maceration. Pancreatin digestion of northern pikeminnow gut contents works because a northern pikeminnow's stomach digests at a high pH, leaving the mineral content of bones untouched. Bass, walleye, and other piscivorous fish use acidic digestion, which demineralizes prey fish bones leaving flaccid wisps that are completely dissolved by pancreatin. Therefore, bass and walleye diets were preserved in ethanol and analyzed apart from northern pikeminnow diets.

A major difference in the two methodologies is that prey fish are identified by diagnostic bones post-pancreatin digestion for northern pikeminnow and, therefore, are not identifiable into more distinct categories (such as salmonid, non-salmonid) for pre-digestion prey weights. Northern pikeminnow diets were macerated with pancreatin and sodium sulfide nonahydrate between 40°C and 45°C. Pancreatin digests most tissue, but does not disintegrate or emulsify fat completely. A 1.5- to 2.0-molar solution of NaOH (lye) was, therefore, used to dissolve the remaining fat. Next, samples were rinsed through a 425-μm (#40) mesh sieve. The diagnostic bones we used to identify and to enumerate fishes (cleithra, dentaries, hyomandibular arches, pharyngeal arches, otoliths, and opercles) are paired structures on the left and right sides of the fish. Therefore, bones were counted in pairs so as not to inflate the number of fish counted. For example, if we counted three left and two right salmon or steelhead cleithra of the same size, the total number of fish was recorded as three. For each individual northern pikeminnow diet that contained fish, the proportion of each prey fish count post-maceration was averaged to represent the mean percent composition of all diets analyzed.

Diet contents were separated into five categories: fish, crayfish, mollusks, insects, and miscellaneous (unidentifiable material, and vegetation /inorganics) and weighed. The most common item in northern pikeminnow stomachs is the miscellaneous category, consisting primarily of a mucilaginous substance that presumably is digesta and sloughed intestinal intima. Each prey category was compiled and weighed for each northern pikeminnow pre-maceration; after weighing, all diet items were returned to the sample bag to be macerated. Prey items in smallmouth bass and walleye diets were identified to the lowest practical taxon and blotted wet weights were recorded.

For each individual predator diet, the proportion of each prey item weight was averaged to represent the mean percent composition of all diets analyzed. Prey items were further identified in each prey category, wherever possible. Prey fish categories included: Unknown fish species, Unknown salmonids, Unknown non-salmonids, Chinook, Whitefish spp., Salmon/Steelhead, Northern Pikeminnow, Peamouth, Chiselmouth, Redside Shiner, Dace spp., Cyprinid spp., *Cottus* spp., Threespine Stickleback, Sucker spp., Walleye, *Lampetra* spp., Sandroller, and *Lepomis* spp. The unknown salmonid group consists of fish that could not be further identified and could include salmon, trout, char, or whitefish. The salmon/steelhead group includes fish in the genus *Oncorhynchus*. Fish in that group cannot be identified beyond genus because their diagnostic bones are too similar. Chinook salmon were only identified as such because of the presence of coded wire tags or PIT tags. Zooplankton diet categories included: *Daphnia* spp., Bosminidae, Chydoridae, Copepoda, Ostracoda, and Sididae. Insect diet categories included: Insect parts, Diptera, Trichoptera, Lepidoptera, Ephemeroptera, Odonata, Orthoptera, Hemiptera, Hymenoptera, Coleoptera, Plecoptera, and unknown insects. Other diet items include: Amphipoda, Isopoda, Mollusca, Annelida, and Arachnida. For each individual predator diet that contained fish, the proportion of each prey fish was averaged to represent the mean percent composition of all diets analyzed.

Data Analyses

Analysis of the data was organized into study year, data collection methodology (that is, Burley and Poe or predator indexing), and sampling period (such as overall, spring, and summer), as defined in the section, "Sample Allocation." Metrics for relative abundance, consumption, and predation were calculated for these periods using the methodology described below for northern pikeminnow and smallmouth bass. Because so few other predators (such as walleye, largemouth bass, and channel catfish) were captured during our efforts, and those that were captured were from a limited geographic area, we determined that developing consumption or predation indices for these species was of limited utility.

Relative Abundance Indices

To estimate the relative abundance indices of northern pikeminnow (> 250 mm) for the Burley and Poe efforts, the density index (DI_{BandP}) was estimated as the proportion of nonzero catches (Counihan and others, 1999). To compare this index to the original values presented in Burley and Poe (1994), we calculated the proportion of nonzero catches from the density index they used:

$$1/\sqrt{proportion\ of\ effort\ with\ zero\ catch} \quad (1)$$

For all other efforts, we estimated the relative abundance of predatory fish by estimating the *CPUE* (number captured per 10 min of electrofishing) of northern pikeminnow (> 170 mm), smallmouth bass (> 150 mm), and walleye (> 180 mm) as the DI_{CPUE} (Ward and others, 1995). The abundance index (*AI*) for each species was then estimated to be:

$$AI_i = DI_i \times S_i \tag{2}$$

where:

AI_i = Index of predator abundance in sampling area *i*,
DI_i = Index of predator density in the sampling area *i*, and
S_i = Surface area (ha) for sampling area *i*, adjusted to include shoreline areas less than 3 m in depth.

To compare our results with those of Burley and Poe, we recalculated the abundance indices they presented based on current estimates of S_i. Estimates of S_i were derived using the GIS of the study area to estimate the area within each of the strata sampled in 2009–10 that are less than 3 m in depth (table 1).

Consumption Indices

Previous studies have demonstrated the analytical techniques we used to develop consumption indices for northern pikeminnow (CI_{NPM}) and smallmouth bass CI_{SBM} (Ward and others, 1995; Ward and Zimmerman, 1999). Ward and others (1995) based their consumption index on the concept of meal turnover-time (Windell, 1978; Rieman and others, 1991). We adopted the methods of Ward and others (1995) to estimate consumption of juvenile salmonids by northern pikeminnow, using the following consumption index:

$$CI_{NPM} = 0.0209 \cdot T^{1\,60} \cdot W^{0\,27} \cdot (n \cdot GW^{-0\,61}) \tag{3}$$

where:

T = water temperature (°C),
W = predator weight (g),
GW = mean total gut weight (g), and
n = mean number of salmonids per northern pikeminnow.

We used the consumption index developed by Ward and Zimmerman (1999), who modified the relations developed by Rogers and Burley (1991) to describe smallmouth bass evacuation time as the consumption index for smallmouth bass as:

$$CI_{SMB} = 0.0407 \left(e^{0\,15T} \cdot W^{0\,23} \cdot \left(n \cdot GW^{-0\,29} \right) \right) \tag{4}$$

where:

T = water temperature (°C),
W = predator weight (g),
GW = mean total gut weight (g), and
n = mean number of salmonids per smallmouth bass.

Predation Indices

We then combined the consumption indices with the abundance indices to calculate the predation index (Ward and others, 1995) as:

$$PI_i = AI_i \cdot CI_i \qquad (5)$$

where:

PI_i = predation index for sample i,
AI_i = abundance index for area i, and
CI_i = consumption index for sample i.

For the comparisons to Burley and Poe, the PI_i was estimated according to the procedures in their report (Burley and Poe, 1994). The predation index values for the predator index sampling in 2009 and 2010 were estimated for each electrofishing effort and then averaged by strata. Reservoir-wide estimates were summed across strata as done by Burley and Poe (1994) and as a mean for a stratified random sample as done by Cochran (1977) for the predator index sampling in 2009 and 2010.

Bioenergetics

The advent of bioenergetics modeling has enabled researchers to estimate the impacts of predators on biota within a system (Hanson and others, 1997). Using data from standard food habit studies that examine instantaneous diets, bioenergetics modeling allows a researcher to estimate energetic requirements of individual or predator cohorts (Brandt and Hartman, 1993). We used the Fish Bioenergetics 3.0 model (Hanson and others, 1997) to estimate prey consumption for northern pikeminnow and smallmouth bass of different ages during spring and summer periods. The bioenergetics model uses the following input parameters: water temperature, predator diet, prey energy density, predator size (weight), predator abundance, and predator age distribution, and works on the generalized formula:
Energy consumed = Respiration + Waste + Growth.
This can be further divided into a more specific mass balance equation (Hanson and others, 1997):
Consumption = (respiration + active metabolism + specific dynamic action) + (egestion + excretion) + (somatic growth + gonad production).
The Fish Bioenergetics software (Hanson and others, 1997) contains many parameter sets for different fishes, but lacks the parameters necessary to model the bioenergetics of northern pikeminnow. Petersen and Ward (1999) compiled the physiological parameters necessary to model the energetic requirement of northern pikeminnow for various situations. Using the available parameters, we constructed model simulations in the Fish Bioenergetics software for northern pikeminnow in the PRP. The model output is based on total weight of prey items consumed by each predator cohort. For our modeling simulations, a cohort is a group of fish of the same age class and species, and the modeled population output is the sum of all individual cohort model runs for each species.

Temporal, biological, and environmental parameters are required to fully populate the bioenergetics model. To estimate the energetic requirement of the fish species evaluated during our study period, water temperature data were obtained from the Grant County Public Utility District Natural Resource link (*http://www.gcpud.org/naturalResources/fishWaterWildlife/waterqualityMonitoring.html*). The diet composition of individual predators throughout the study period was obtained from our field collections. The proportion of a diet for an individual was calculated by dividing the sum of each individual prey item by the total weight of the diet contents for that individual. Diet data from field collections were compiled by day, species, and age class, and were averaged for each model day. Diet contents were then assigned constant energy densities using various literature sources (Cummins and Wuycheck, 1971; Stewart and others, 1983). For model simulations, we estimated the Bioenergetics software p-value (proportion of maximum consumption) based on hypothetical consumption rates that would likely have been experienced in the field. We used a p-value of 0.5 for both smallmouth bass and northern pikeminnow in the PRP and conducted model runs assuming fish consumed 50 percent of their maximum consumption rate. Values commonly range between 0.2 and 0.6 estimated from observed growth of fishes in the field for bioenergetics modeling (Dieterman and others, 2004; Mateo, 2007; McCarthy and others, 2009).

We used our estimated ages of the fish collected to partition the proportion of the modeled population into age classes (table 2) or individual cohorts for the bioenergetics modeling. The age data was further used to determine mean length at age, and the mean weight of each age class for both smallmouth bass and northern pikeminnow. Because we did not have an accurate population estimate for the species of interest, we used our field data to estimate a hypothetical population for modeling purposes. The total numbers of predators captured were used for the population estimate. Modeling was further partitioned into spring and summer periods for the 2009 and 2010 study years, relative to our study periods based on juvenile salmonid migration times.

Results

River Conditions

River discharge and water temperatures in 2009 were lower than the 10-year average from mid-June to early-July, and remained lower than the 10-year average for the remainder of the field season (fig. 3). Conversely, in 2010, river discharge generally was higher from mid-June to early-July, and consistently higher than the 10-year average. Water temperatures in 2009–10 were similar to the 10-year average.

Catch Data

Northern Pikeminnow

Northern pikeminnow were captured during 2009 Burley and Poe sampling efforts, and also during 2009 and 2010 predator index sampling efforts. During the Burley and Poe sampling, we captured and measured 1,225 northern pikeminnow ranging from 43 to 580 mm in total length in Priest Rapids and Wanapum Reservoirs (fig. 4). Similar overall numbers of fish were captured between the spring (n=601) and summer (n=624) periods. The fish captured during the spring period, ranging from 43 to 531 mm in total length, were slightly smaller than fish captured during the summer efforts, ranging from 50 to 580 mm in total length. The *CPUE* of northern pikeminnow greater than 250 mm in total length during the 2009 Burley and Poe sampling was highest in the Rock Island tailrace and generally was higher in Wanapum reservoir than in Priest Rapids reservoir for both spring and summer periods (table 3).

The predator index sampling during 2009 covered a longer time period (overall, May 1–August 27) than during Burley and Poe, but fewer fish were captured (n=1,025). The northern pikeminnow captured ranged from 40 to 567 mm in total length (fig. 5); smaller than those captured during Burley and Poe efforts. During the spring, we captured 392 northern pikeminnow ranging from 45 to 520 mm in total length. Fewer fish were captured during the summer (n=361), but the overall total lengths were larger, as seen during the Burley and Poe sampling (ranging from 61 to 539 mm in total length) (fig. 5). The *CPUE* of northern pikeminnow greater than 170 mm during 2009 predator index sampling was highest in Rock Island tailrace during the spring, and generally was higher in the Wanapum reservoir than in the Priest Rapids reservoir during the spring and summer periods (table 3).

Sampling started and ended later in 2010 than in 2009. However, we captured and measured the greatest number of northern pikeminnow in 2010 compared to all other sampling efforts (n=2,581). The northern pikeminnow captured ranged from 33 to 581 mm in total length (fig. 6). During the spring period, we captured 544 northern pikeminnow ranging from 42 to 510 mm in total length; in the summer period, we captured almost double that number with 990 northern pikeminnow ranging from 42 to 581 mm in total length (fig. 6). The *CPUE* of northern pikeminnow greater than 170 mm in total length during the 2010 spring period was highest in the Priest Rapids tailrace near-BRZ reach, followed by the Wanapum mid-reservoir (table 4). For the summer period, the *CPUE* was highest in the Wanapum mid-reservoir followed by the Priest Rapids tailrace near-BRZ reach.

The mean lengths of northern pikeminnow captured during sampling efforts varied by strata in the PRP (figs. 7–9). Generally, we found that larger northern pikeminnow were more prevalent near the dams than in the mid-reservoir reaches. During the Burley and Poe sampling, the largest mean northern pikeminnow lengths were from fish in the forebay of Wanapum Dam and the tailrace of Priest Rapids Dam (fig. 7). This trend was evident in both the spring and summer periods. For the 2009 and 2010 predator indexing efforts, the largest mean northern pikeminnow lengths were from fish in the tailrace and forebay of Wanapum Dam and in the tailrace of Priest Rapids Dam (figs. 8 and 9).

Aging analysis was completed for all northern pikeminnow (fig. 10) captured in 2009, 2010, and 2011 in the PRP. The analysis indicated that ages of the captured fish ranged from 1 to 24 years (median age = 3 years). The mean length at age was estimated for all age classes (fig. 11). For all northern pikeminnow captured in the Priest Rapids reservoir, the relationship between length and weight is described by the equation:

$$\log_{10} (\text{weight}) = 2.9974(\log_{10} \text{length}) - 5.1203; \ r^2 = 0.9625;$$

For Wanapum Reservoir the relation is described by:

$$\log_{10} (\text{weight}) = 3.0422(\log_{10} \text{length}) - 5.2224; \ r^2 = 0.9813.$$

Smallmouth bass

We captured smallmouth bass in the PRP during the Burley and Poe efforts in 2009 and during the predator indexing efforts in 2009 and 2010. We generally captured fewer smallmouth bass than northern pikeminnow for all sampling efforts. We captured and measured 272 smallmouth bass during the Burley and Poe sampling in the PRP ranging from 35 to 518 mm in total length (fig. 12). In the spring, we captured 168 smallmouth bass ranging from 51 to 517 mm in total length and in the summer, we captured 104 smallmouth bass ranging from 35 to 518 mm in total length. The *CPUE* of smallmouth bass greater 150 mm in length in the spring and summer Burley and Poe sampling was highest in the forebay of Priest Rapids Dam and in the mid-reservoir section of Priest Rapids Reservoir (table 3).

Fewer smallmouth bass were captured in the 2009 predator indexing sampling than during the Burley and Poe sampling. During predator index sampling, we captured 232 smallmouth bass in Priest Rapids and Wanapum Reservoirs that ranged from 21 to 479 mm in total length (fig. 13). In the spring, we captured 48 bass that ranged from 105 to 467 mm in total length. The capture number more than doubled for the summer period (n=112), with smallmouth bass that ranged from 112 to 450 mm in total length (fig. 13). The *CPUE* for predator indexing was highest in the forebay BRZs of Priest Rapids and Wanapum Dams in the spring and summer periods (table 3).

The 2010 sampling resulted in the highest number of smallmouth bass being captured out of all the sampling efforts; this followed the same trend as the northern pikeminnow capture results. We captured and measured 687 smallmouth bass ranging from 46 to 515 mm in total length in Priest Rapids and Wanapum Reservoirs (fig. 14). In the spring sampling, we captured 149 bass ranging from 71 to 469 mm in total length; in the summer sampling, we captured 294 bass ranging from 73 to 515 mm in total length (fig. 14). The *CPUE* of smallmouth bass greater than 150 mm in length in the spring and summer periods was highest in the forebay areas of Priest Rapids and Wanapum Dams (table 4).

We also observed spatial trends in the mean length of smallmouth bass captured across the strata sampled in 2009 and 2010 (figs. 15–17). During Burley and Poe spring 2009 sampling, the largest mean smallmouth bass lengths were from the tailrace and forebay of Wanapum Dam and the tailrace of Priest Rapids Dam (fig. 15). A similar trend was evident in the Burley and Poe summer sampling with the exception that only one bass was captured in the Priest Rapids tailrace. For the 2009 and 2010 predator index sampling, the largest mean smallmouth bass lengths were from the Priest Rapids mid-reservoir and tailrace reaches, and the Wanapum forebay and mid-reservoir reaches (figs. 16 and 17).

Our aging analyses of smallmouth bass (fig. 18) captured in 2009, 2010, and 2011, in the Priest Rapids Project indicate that the ages ranged from 1 to 14 years (median age = 3 years). The mean length at age was estimated for smallmouth bass and is presented in figure 19. For all smallmouth bass captured in Priest Rapids Reservoir, the relation between length and weight is described by the equation:

$$\log_{10} (\text{weight}) = 3.1151(\log_{10} \text{length}) - 5.1566; \ r^2 = 0.9864;$$

for Wanapum Reservoir, the relation is described by:

$$\log_{10} (\text{weight}) = 3.1417(\log_{10} \text{length}) - 5.2164; \ r^2 = 0.9829.$$

Walleye

Very few walleye were captured across all sampling efforts and study years. During the Burley and Poe sampling, we captured 13 walleye in Priest Rapids and Wanapum Reservoirs, ranging from 100 to 775 mm in total length (fig. 20). In the spring, we captured seven walleye that ranged from 425 to 775 mm in total length; in the summer, we captured six walleye that ranged from 100 to 481 mm in total length. During the 2009 predator index sampling, we captured 18 walleye in Priest Rapids and Wanapum Reservoirs that ranged from 165 to 685 mm in total length (fig. 21). Of these only 3 walleye were captured in the spring period, while 15 walleye were captured in the summer, ranging from 165 to 685 mm in total length (fig. 21). We captured more than three times as many walleye in 2010 (n=59), ranging from 184 to 786 mm in total length (fig. 22). In the spring 2010 predator index sampling, we captured 15 walleye ranging from 200 to 771 mm in total length, and in the summer, we captured 21 walleye ranging from 194 to 693 mm in total length (fig. 22). The *CPUE* for walleye was low in both the spring and summer for all sampling periods (< 0.005) in 2009 and 2010, with the highest values from the Priest Rapids BRZ (*CPUE* = 0.01) in both the spring and summer.

Our aging analyses of walleye (fig. 23) captured in 2009, 2010, and 2011 in the Priest Rapids Project indicate that walleye ages range from 1 to 16 years (median age = 3 years; *n*=34). The mean length at age relation for walleye is described in figure 24. We did not develop a relationship between length and weight or examine the spatial variability in mean lengths because so few walleye were captured.

Diet Analyses

Northern Pikeminnow

When we evaluated the diets of northern pikeminnow, we found the highest proportion of the diet was consistently the miscellaneous prey category. That is, the highest proportion by weight could not be identified into any of the other prey categories during the pre-maceration process. Of the diets collected as part of the Burley and Poe spring sampling, the miscellaneous prey category constituted on average 59 percent, with insects as the next dominant item at 31 percent, followed by fish (6 percent), mollusks, and crayfish (fig. 25). The diets from the Priest Rapids tailrace reach had the highest percentage of fish (18 percent) in the spring sampling, followed by the Priest Rapids forebay (10 percent), and Rock Island tailrace (6 percent). For the summer sampling, the diet proportions were similar to the spring with 61 percent as miscellaneous, 30 percent insects, and 6 percent mollusks, followed by fish (1.5 percent) and crayfish (fig. 25). The proportion of fish (6.5 percent) was highest in the tailrace of Rock Island Dam in the summer (fig. 25). Of the diets with fish prey items captured during Burley and Poe sampling, northern pikeminnow containing salmon occurred in four strata in the spring (Priest Rapids tailrace, Wanapum tailrace, Wanapum forebay, and Wanapum mid-reservoir), and no salmon were observed in the diets in the summer.

In the 2009 predator index sampling, we observed similar trends with fish constituting a relatively minor component of the diets of northern pikeminnow captured, but being more prevalent near the dams (fig. 26). Sampling fish comprised on average 2 percent of the diet in the spring and 3 percent in the summer. Percentages of fish prey items were highest in the Wanapum forebay BRZ (11 percent) in the spring, and in the tailraces of Priest Rapids (13 percent) and Wanapum (13 percent) dams (fig. 26) in the summer. Of the northern pikeminnow with fish in their diets, salmon were present in low proportions in the Priest Rapids tailrace only in spring (0.44) and summer (0.25).

Although fish were a relatively minor component of the northern pikeminnow diet in the 2010 predator index sampling, they were again most prevalent in the diets of northern pikeminnow captured in the reaches nearest to Priest Rapids, Wanapum, and Rock Island Dams (fig. 27). In the spring sampling, the average proportion of the diet consisting of fish (16 percent) was higher than in all of the 2009 sampling efforts. However, the most dominant prey items were still in the miscellaneous category (61 percent), followed by insects (19 percent), and then fish, mollusks, and crayfish. In the summer, the average proportion of diet consisting of fish was much lower (1.1 percent), with most reaches sampled having no northern pikeminnow captured with fish in their diets (fig. 27). The proportion of the fish prey that was salmon in northern pikeminnow was variable among strata, and was highest in the tailrace of Wanapum Dam (fig. 28). The occurrence of salmon within the fish prey items generally was higher in the tailrace areas than in the forebay and mid-reservoir areas, and was higher in the spring than in the summer (fig. 28).

Smallmouth Bass

The diets of smallmouth bass generally had a much higher proportion of fish prey items than northern pikeminnow diets. For smallmouth bass collected during the spring Burley and Poe sampling, fish constituted the highest percentage (84 percent) on average of the diet. The same result was seen for the summer sampling, with fish constituting an average of 67 percent of the smallmouth bass diet. This trend was consistent across most of the reaches sampled in the spring and summer periods, with the exception of the Priest Rapids forebay (fig. 29). Of the smallmouth bass diets with fish, salmon were documented only in the Priest Rapids mid-reservoir reach in the spring.

During the 2009 predator index sampling, fish generally were generally the most prevalent diet item in smallmouth bass. On average, fish were 55 percent of the spring smallmouth bass diet, and 76 percent of their summer diet. Fish were the most prevalent smallmouth bass diet item in all reaches where diets were collected, with the exception of the Priest Rapids tailrace BRZ (fig. 30). Juvenile salmonids were found in the diets of bass collected in the forebay of Priest Rapids Dam and in the Priest Rapids mid-reservoir reach in the spring. In the summer, salmon were found in the diets of bass collected in four reaches: Priest Rapids tailrace, Priest Rapids forebay, Priest Rapids mid-reservoir, and Wanapum mid-reservoir. In all cases, the proportion of fish in the diets that were salmon never exceeded 0.25.

As in the 2009 sampling, fish generally were the dominant prey item for smallmouth bass captured in 2010 (fig. 31). On average, fish were 83 percent of the diet in the spring and 57 percent of the diet in the summer. This trend was consistent across all reaches with the exception of crayfish that were the dominant prey item in the summer in the forebay BRZs for both Priest Rapids and Wanapum Dams. fig. 31). Salmonids were observed in the diets of smallmouth bass captured in eight reaches concentrated in the forebays and mid-reservoir reaches of Priest Rapids and Wanapum Dams in 2010.

Walleye

The diets of walleye, collected during the Burley and Poe sampling and the 2009 and 2010 predator index sampling, consisted primarily of fish. The proportion of fish in the diets was mostly near 1, with the exception of a fish collected in the Rock Island tailrace reach in 2009 that had no fish in its stomach. Otherwise, the proportion of walleye diets that were fish was never less than 0.89. The proportion of fish in the diets of walleye that were salmon was concentrated in the tailrace of Priest Rapids Dam, and ranged from 0.5 to -1. In 2010, the distribution of walleye collected that had salmon was higher (fig. 32). The proportion of salmon in the diets of walleye captured in 2010 was highest in the tailrace of Priest Rapids Dam in the spring and in the tailrace of Wanapum Dam in the summer (fig. 32).

Predation Indices

Northern Pikeminnow

Northern pikeminnow predation indices estimated for the Burley and Poe sampling were very low, and were much lower than those estimated in 1993 (Burley and Poe, 1994). Predation index values for 2009 ranged from 0 to 31 in the spring, and no predation was evident in samples from the summer (table 5). The predation index estimates we calculated based on the data from Burley and Poe (1994) ranged from 0 to 71 in the spring and 0 to 120 in the summer. For the 2009 predator index sampling, the estimated predation indices that used *CPUE* as the density index also indicated very low predation in the study area in the spring and summer with only the Priest Rapids tailrace being greater than zero (table 6). The northern pikeminnow predation indices for 2010 were higher and more widely distributed throughout the study area than in 2009, ranging from 0 to 1.918 (table 7). Northern pikeminnow predation in 2010 was highest in the Wanapum mid-reservoir (1.918, SE=1.211) and Wanapum tailrace (1.018, SE=1.018) reaches in the spring, and were less than 0.196 in the summer with evidence of predation occurring only in the Rock Island tailrace and the Priest Rapids mid-reservoir reaches.

Smallmouth Bass

The predation indices for smallmouth bass during the 2009 predator index sampling indicated that predation of salmonids in the study area was low in all areas in the spring and summer (table 6). In the spring, predation indices were less than 0.240 for all reaches, and predation of salmonids was documented in the Priest Rapids mid-reservoir and the Priest Rapids forebay reaches (PF1 and PF0) only. For the summer, predation of salmonids was documented in the Priest Rapids tailrace near-BRZ, the Priest Rapids mid-reservoir, the Priest Rapids forebay BRZ, and the Wanapum mid-reservoir, with the highest index value from the Priest Rapids tailrace (1.073, SE=1.073). In 2010, our results suggest that predation of juvenile salmonids by smallmouth bass was more widespread than in 2009 (table 7). In the spring of 2010, predation was highest in the Priest Rapids mid-reservoir reach (5.940, SE 2.731), followed by the Wanapum forebay BRZ (0.90, SE=0.90) and the Priest Rapids forebay near-BRZ reach (0.114, SE=0.114). In the summer, predation was again highest in the Priest Rapids mid-reservoir (1.760, SE=1.152), the Priest Rapids forebay reach (1.055, SE=0.776), and the Wanapum forebay BRZ and near-BRZ reaches. In the spring and summer, predation was higher in the forebay and mid-reservoir reaches than in the tailraces.

Bioenergetics

We observed seasonal differences in total and fish consumption by northern pikeminnow and smallmouth bass in 2009 and 2010. The output from the bioenergetics model results indicated that the northern pikeminnow modeled population (n=928) consumed 6,447 g of fish in the spring 2009 (fig. 33), which was approximately 15 percent of their diet by weight (fig. 34). In the summer, the weight of fish consumed (5,002 g) was 3 percent less than in the spring sampling period. In 2010, the modeled population (n=1,118) consumed 11,865 g of fish in the spring (9 percent of their diet) (fig. 34) and 20,995 g in the summer (fig. 33). Even though the proportion of the modeled population diet that was composed of fish was only 3 percent, the total grams of fish consumed by northern pikeminnow in the summer, was much higher (fig. 34).

A higher proportion of the diets of smallmouth bass were composed of fish than northern pikeminnow. We estimated smallmouth bass (n=165) consumed 1,124 g of fish in spring 2009 and 4,192 g in summer 2009 (fig. 35). This comprised approximately 60 and 40 percent of their total diet (fig. 36). We further estimated that 168 g (9 percent of diet) of salmonids were consumed in the spring and 801 g (8 percent of diet) in the summer. In 2010, the modeled population of smallmouth bass (n=372) consumed 1,582 grams (55 percent of diet) of fish in the spring and 12,448 g (48 percent of diet) in the summer. The salmonid consumption was estimated to be 354 g (12 percent of diet) in the spring and 2,667 g (11 percent of diet) in the summer.

Discussion

The predation indices estimated from the Burley and Poe sampling in 2009 were much lower than those we calculated from the 1993 data of Burley and Poe (1994). This may be a result of efforts to reduce the abundance of northern pikeminnow in the Priest Rapids project by physically capturing and removing them (Garner and Keeler, 2008). The reduced predation may be, in part, a result of changes in the northern pikeminnow population characteristics brought about by the northern pikeminnow removal program. The mean total lengths we observed in the study reaches were much lower than those reported in Burley and Poe (1994). For instance, Burley and Poe (1994) reported a mean fork length of 436 mm for northern pikeminnow captured in the Wanapum Dam tailrace; the mean total length of northern pikeminnow we captured in this reach was less than 150 mm in both the spring and summer periods. Grant PUD also has noted a decrease in the average size of northern pikeminnow captured in 2011 compared to previous years but note that the reduction may be due to gear bias (Curt Dotson, Grant County Public Utility District, written communication 2011). However, our results summarizing data from northern pikeminnow captured using a different gear, electrofishing, corroborate Grant PUD's observations.

Reductions in the size of northern pikeminnow may be resulting in a decrease in predation because consumption of juvenile salmonids increases with the size of northern pikeminnow (Vigg and others, 1991). Rieman and Beamesderfer (1991) suggest that continuous exploitation of northern pikeminnow greater than 250 mm in fork length would result in a 50 percent or greater reduction in predation. When evaluating the effects of the pikeminnow removal program, Zimmerman and Ward (1999) documented post-removal program predation index values that were 44–91 percent lower than mean values prior to the implementation of the removal program throughout the lower Columbia River basin. Zimmerman and Ward (1999) note that the observed declines in relative predation were consistent with changes in the size and age structure of northern pikeminnow populations associated with the Northern Pikeminnow Management Program; that is, there was a shift towards smaller, younger individuals (Knutsen and Ward, 1999). Although the overall mean size of northern pikeminnow captured as part of our electrofishing efforts has decreased compared to 1993, we observed similar trends in mean length in the longitudinal reaches. Specifically, we observed a trend of larger fish in reaches nearest the dams, as did Burley and Poe (1994), suggesting that larger fish within the population still are found near dams. Our analysis of the diets of northern pikeminnow also suggests that the fish captured near Wanapum and Priest Rapids Dams were more likely to have fish as a component of their diets, and that salmon were found in their diets.

Very low northern pikeminnow predation indices were observed in 2009 for both the Burley and Poe and the predator index sampling, despite differences in the diel timing of these efforts. The electrofishing efforts conducted during the predator indexing began no earlier than 30 min after sunset, while the Burley and Poe electrofishing began 90 min before sunrise and continued sampling until a target catch of 15 northern pikeminnow were captured from each section sampled. That a similar result was attained for the different approaches suggests that the low levels of predation observed during the 2009 Burley and Poe efforts were not a function of the timing of the sampling. Although conducting electrofishing at night during the 2009 and 2010 predator index sampling versus early-morning resulted in a higher *CPUE* in most reaches and seasons for both northern pikeminnow and smallmouth bass, the increased collections did not result in higher predation index values. Furthermore, the timing of the summer 2009 Burley and Poe efforts were conducted past the peak migration period for sub-yearling Chinook salmon. Another factor that may have affected our results was that we were tagging and releasing northern pikeminnow with the intent of recapturing them; which occurred infrequently enough that we discontinued the efforts in 2010. Because there were so few northern pikeminnow captured in 2009 that were in the larger size categories, releasing the few we did capture likely resulted in us releasing predators that were the most likely to contain salmonids in their diets. The release of predators as part of our tagging effort could have contributed to the lack of documented predation in the summer 2009. However, there was little evidence of predation from our sampling efforts in the summer 2010 in many of the reaches.

We observed a shift in the diet composition of northern pikeminnow collected in the PRP from 1993 to the present (2011). Burley and Poe (1994) reported that the average proportion of northern pikeminnow diet that was fish was 0.66 in the spring and 0.35 in the summer; the largest proportion we observed was less than 0.2. The shift towards insects and food items other than fish may be a reflection of the reduction in the average size of northern pikeminnow captured; the shift is not likely the result of a reduced prey base because of the constant supply of hatchery juvenile salmonids migrating through the PRP. The ecological implications of the shift to a greater portion of northern pikeminnow being smaller are unclear and beyond the scope of this report. However, if our observations are indicative of the diets of most of the northern pikeminnow population in the study area, than it seems reasonable to assume that there would be consequences of a shift away from piscivory.

The results of our study suggest that there are areas within the PRP that can be targeted to mitigate the predation of smallmouth bass on juvenile salmonids. However, our results do not suggest that juvenile salmonids were a major constituent in the diet of smallmouth bass. Despite the higher proportion of fish observed in the diets of smallmouth bass, the predation indices during the 2009 predator index sampling supplied little evidence to suggest that juvenile salmonid predation by bass was very prevalent in the study area. The fact that juvenile salmon do not constitute a significant portion of the diet of smallmouth bass also has been observed in other studies. For instance, Naughton and others (2004) observed that juvenile salmonids constituted a maximum of 11 percent of the diets of smallmouth bass captured in the forebay of the Lower Granite Dam, Snake River, and only 5 percent in other areas of the Snake and Clearwater Rivers. Similar to our results for northern pikeminnow, predation indices were higher and more widespread throughout the study area for smallmouth bass in spring 2010 than in 2009. However, dissimilar to what we observed for northern pikeminnow, predation was high and more widespread in summer 2010 suggesting that smallmouth bass predation of sub-yearling Chinook salmon may be higher than predation of northern pikeminnow. In 2010, predation by smallmouth bass was highest in the Priest Rapids mid-reservoir reach and concentrated in the forebay areas of Priest Rapids and Wanapum Dams. Similarly, Naughton and others (2004) observed that the highest monthly consumption rates of juvenile salmonids by smallmouth bass were in the forebay areas in April 1996 and in the forebay BRZ in July 1997 at Lower Granite Dam, Snake River. Our findings also agree with those of Vigg and others (1991), who found that in the John Day Reservoir, Columbia River, consumption of juvenile salmonids by smallmouth bass was highest in the forebay. Ward and Zimmerman (1999), who found smallmouth bass consumption of juvenile salmonids usually was highest in the summer in the forebay of John Day Reservoir, and also was evident downstream of Bonneville Dam (rkm 190–197). Ward and Zimmerman (1999) also observed that consumption of juvenile salmonids by smallmouth bass was highly variable across reservoir reaches (for example forebay, mid-reservoir, and tailrace areas) and seasons and generally was low.

The results of our diet analyses for smallmouth bass suggest that fish were a more significant constituent in the diets of smallmouth bass compared to northern pikeminnow. Our diet analysis results are consistent with those previously reported for the study area. Burley and Poe (1994) reported that the diets of smallmouth bass collected in their survey of the mid-Columbia River consisted of 87 percent fish, 12 percent crustaceans, and 1 percent other items. The diet composition of smallmouth bass collected in the study area, however, seems to differ from the observed diets of smallmouth bass collected in other reaches of the Columbia and Snake Rivers, where smallmouth bass are relatively more abundant. Specifically, smallmouth bass in other reaches of the Columbia and Snake Rivers have been shown to contain a higher percentage of crustaceans. For instance, Naughton and others (2004) reported that crustaceans comprised the highest percentage of the diet (by weight) of smallmouth bass 175–249 mm in total length at all locations they sampled in the Snake River in 1996 and 1997, except for the Clearwater River arm, where non-salmonid fishes were the primary prey item. For smallmouth bass 250–389 mm in total length, Naughton and others (2004) observed that crustaceans were the primary diet item in 1997. Burley and Poe (1994) reported that crustaceans constituted 42 percent of the dietary totals for smallmouth bass collected in the John Day Reservoir. Zimmerman (1999) also found that in spring and summer, the proportional weight of crayfish was highest in the impounded reaches of the Columbia (50 percent) and Snake (52 percent) Rivers. From the results reported from other areas of the Columbia and Snake Rivers, crustaceans appear to be an important diet item of smallmouth bass. If the diets of smallmouth bass we collected are reflective of the availability of crustaceans as prey items in the study area, perhaps the lack of crustaceans available as prey may be limiting smallmouth bass numbers in the study area. Low densities of crayfish, for instance, could be due to a lack of suitable habitat in the study area or predation by another fish species, such as the northern pikeminnow.

Low numbers of walleye have been reported by other researchers sampling fishes in the Priest Rapids Project. Despite sampling the study area for approximately 4 months during each of 2009 and 2010 with electrofishing gear, we captured very few walleye. Burley and Poe (1994) captured only 16 walleye in the study area during their sampling efforts in 1993. Electrofishing may be inefficient at capturing walleye. Schoenebeck and Hansen (2005) suggest that the relationship between electrofishing catch rates and population size may depend on habitat and may vary seasonally. However, Rogers and others (2003) found that the electrofishing catch rate of adult walleye was positively related to adult walleye density, and that the electrofishing catch rate of the total walleye population was positively related to total walleye density. In a study that examined the fish population structure in the Priest Rapids Project, only 35 walleye were captured despite their efforts to capture fish with various gear in addition to electrofishing gear (Pfeifer and others, 2001). Our catches suggest little walleye recruitment is occurring in the study area. Pfeifer and others (2001) collected some smaller individuals in the backwaters of the Wanapum reservoir and hypothesized that walleye may have spawned successfully in the reservoir or recruited from upstream sources, principally Lake Roosevelt; our catch data lead us to concur with this assessment.

Our bioenergetics modeling provided additional insight into the interactions of predators and juvenile salmonids in the study area. The bioenergetics modeling output indicates that fish (in general) and salmon (in particular) consumed by weight were greater in the summer than in the spring sampling periods, with the exception of the 2009 northern pikeminnow data; despite the results that the proportion of fish in the diets of northern pikeminnow and smallmouth bass were slightly less in the summer. We used daily diets and temperatures based on field-data collections, but held the proportion of maximum consumption constant across the study period as inputs into the bioenergetics model. Given that water temperatures increased in the summer migration period, we expect a concomitant increase in the energetic requirements of northern pikeminnow and smallmouth bass. Increased energetic demands can either be manifested as a loss in weight or an increase in either total consumption or increase in consumption of higher energy density prey items, such as fish to compensate for the higher energy demands. Our results show that northern pikeminnow and smallmouth bass total consumption and fish consumption by weight were higher in the summer periods, suggesting that predation effects from northern pikeminnow and smallmouth bass may be higher for juvenile salmon (namely, sub-yearling Chinook salmon) migrating in the summer sampling period. Our efforts to characterize the diets of northern pikeminnow and smallmouth bass in the study area and couple that information to a bioenergetics framework also could provide a way to assess the effects of existing removal programs, such as the Grant PUD northern pikeminnow removal program or the potential effects of new removal programs, such as those for smallmouth bass. For instance, one could model the predicted reductions in salmon eaten that would occur if a certain number of smallmouth bass were removed. Converting the reductions in the salmon eaten by weight to numbers of salmon would require assumptions regarding the relative proportions of various salmon species in the diet and the size distributions of the species. However, such a modeling exercise would provide context to the relative benefits expected in light of the cost of implementing such a program.

In 2009, our fish collection efforts resulted in the capture of few northern pikeminnow that were large fish (> 250 mm) with salmon in their stomachs. Thus, a result of using this data for bioenergetics modeling is that very few salmonids were consumed relative to other prey items in the modeling scenarios. However, this result is consistent with diet results from the northern pikeminnow removal program studies, where the proportion of northern pikeminnow diets that were smolts ranged from 0.8 to 1.8 percent for study years 2008 and 2009 (Garner and Keeler, 2008, 2009). In 2010, fish and salmon consumption was higher than in 2009, and likely was a result of the collection of more large predators with salmon in their stomachs in 2010. The estimated weight of fish consumed by northern pikeminnow may be underestimated as a result of the differences in their morphology and physiology and the processing of their stomach contents. Much of the material in a northern pikeminnow's stomach often consisted of miscellaneous material, some of which may have been salmonid prey items, but was not discernible during the pre-maceration as fish. Thus, even though salmonids and other fish can be detected in the diets post-maceration, a weight was not assigned to this prey item to be incorporated into the diet by weight analysis. Thus, the fish prey weights are underrepresented in the diet proportions for northern pikeminnow. We chose not to estimate a weight associated with bones found post-maceration, as we did not have a method to consistently assign a weight to these fish such that it would be represented properly with the other items found in the stomach at that time. Smallmouth bass have a true stomach and partitioned digestive tract, making the collection and identification of prey items considerably easier. Furthermore, the focus of this study was on predation indices, which use the counts of salmon found in stomachs to estimate predation and not a proportion of weights of salmon in the diet. In theory, diagnostic bones can be measured and used to estimate the size of a fish prey item at the time of consumption; however, this would then overestimate the weight of fish in the diet relative to the other items in which pre-consumption weights could not be estimated.

Our inability to access the BRZ areas of Priest Rapids and Wanapum Dams during the 2009 Burley and Poe sampling confounds comparisons to the results of the study conducted in 1993. Burley and Poe (1994) observed relatively high consumption index values in the BRZs. Ward and others (1995) and others have observed that predation is disproportionately large near dams, with 33 percent of the overall predation occurring in the BRZs. To attain access to the BRZs, it was necessary to coordinate with the dam operators so that discharge through the spillway could be discontinued to allow our electrofishing crews safe access to these areas. Despite our efforts at coordination, we encountered issues that precluded us from completing scheduled sampling events. In addition to coordination (miscommunication) and logistical issues (river flows that precluded the cessation of spill), during the 2009 and 2010 sampling seasons, we also encountered environmental conditions (such as high winds and river flows) that kept us from sampling the BRZ areas. Although we were unable to access the BRZs as part of the 2009 Burley and Poe sampling, we did have limited success as part of our other sampling efforts in 2009 and 2010.

We recommend that future predation studies in the Priest Rapids Project include a design scheme to allocate sample efforts to areas immediately adjacent to the BRZ areas, such as was done in 2010. The addition of a reach as close to the dam as possible but not in the BRZ allowed us to allocate efforts to areas thought to have higher consumption rates. We recommend retaining these reaches in future studies of predation in the PRP. The logistical constraint and safety issues we encountered trying to sample the BRZ areas biased estimates of these areas and, therefore, our assessment of predation in the study area. Studies examining predation in other reaches of the Columbia River have shown these areas can have high densities of predators (Ward and others, 1995). Evaluations of diets of northern pikeminnow collected off the transformer deck of the Wanapum Dam suggest these fish were more likely to contain salmonids than fish captured in other areas (Hardiman and others, 2012). That the predation indices for smallmouth bass were as high as they were for the forebay areas, especially for Wanapum Dam in the summer 2010 sampling, suggest relatively high levels of predation given the small area contained within that reach. Therefore, although the data we present suggest that predation is lower now (2010) than in 1993, our results suggest areas where control efforts for smallmouth bass could be focused if managers chose this as an action to mitigate the predation losses caused by smallmouth bass. Although our catch data for walleye suggest that this species is not abundant in the study area, our *CPUE* and diet analyses suggest areas where efforts to reduce the numbers of this species could be focused; the tailraces of Priest Rapids and Wanapum Dams are the areas where salmon were documented as being consumed by walleye.

Future predation indexing should either be conducted throughout the migration season, or the migration run timing variability because of environmental conditions or hatchery practices, and whether monitoring for predation of multiple species or of one particular species is desired need to be incorporated into the sampling design. Our efforts to repeat the timing of the 1993 study were confounded by the lack of reported criteria used to time the 1993 fieldwork. We surmised from the Burley and Poe (1994) report that the logistics of conducting such an effort over a large geographical area, much larger than the PRP, dictated to some extent when sampling was conducted in a particular river reach. In the absence of specific criteria, we chose to use water temperature as a criterion to begin sampling. Water temperature was selected as a criterion because of the bioenergetic implications of predator activity associated with changing temperatures (Cech and others, 1994) and our desire to sample under conditions similar to those of the original work. This decision resulted in our Burley and Poe summer sampling period occurring towards the end of the summer migration. Conversely, the 2009 and 2010 predator index sampling was structured so that sampling efforts mostly encompassed both the spring and summer migration periods. Sampling continuously throughout the juvenile salmonid migration in 2009 and 2010 allowed us to use juvenile salmonid passage information to place the predation sampling in the context of the migration of multiple juvenile salmonid species. How to strategize the timing of efforts to characterize predation in a particular area potentially is problematic for future efforts to examine predation in the PRP, especially for the purposes of determining trends over time.

Progress towards the development of a comprehensive long-term monitoring strategy was confounded by the redirect of the original objectives and tasks for the third and final year of this study to address predation of steelhead in 2011 (Hardiman and others, 2012). However, the PRCC has expressed continued interest in establishing a predation monitoring program in the Priest Rapids Project. Toward this end, we provide recommendations on how to proceed with the development of such a program. Monitoring programs that address a diverse set of objectives and information should occur nationwide and provide information on: regulation compliance, the status of aquatic resource conditions, effectiveness of management and regulatory programs, and policy planning and decision-making processes. Considerable expenditures have been made on such programs, often with mixed results and information provided. The U.S. Environmental Protection Agency (EPA) initiated the Environmental Monitoring and Assessment Program (EMAP) to advance the science of natural resource monitoring at regional and national scales. A significant task in the development of EMAP has been the statistical design and analysis methodologies to support meeting the goal of "with known confidence" in the design of monitoring studies. This effort has drawn heavily on existing survey design literature and applications in other areas.

The EPA reviewed past and current aquatic monitoring programs and identified some common characteristics of the design and analyses for such programs that fail—that is, do not meet the expectations for producing information regarding the status and trends of aquatic resources—and generally categorized them into four broad classes.

The objectives for monitoring are not clearly, precisely stated and understood.

Monitoring measurement protocols, survey design, and statistical analysis become scientifically out-of-date.

Monitoring results are not directly tied to management decision-making.

Results are not timely nor communicated to key audiences in terms they can understand.

Organizations such as EPA that conduct national and regional monitoring, and regional groups such as the Pacific Northwest Aquatic Monitoring Partnership (http://www.pnamp.org/) have identified key aquatic resource survey design components necessary for the formulation of a long-term monitoring effort. For instance, the EPA suggests that the following are necessary components for a monitoring program:

- Objectives stated precisely and quantitatively.
- Target population explicitly, precisely defined.
- Sample frame constructed that represents the target population.
- Decision on which survey design will best provide information to meet objectives.
- Selection of sampling sites using survey design.
- Implementation of consistent measurement protocols at sampled sites.
- Statistical analysis that matches survey design.

We suggest that the completion and inclusion of these components are necessary to enact a long-term monitoring activity for predation in the Priest Rapids Project. We strongly recommend that the PRCC pursue the completion of these key elements as they make progress towards the development of long-term monitoring programs.

We further recommend that the PRCC convene an expert panel that can work through the completion of these components. Participation in regional monitoring groups, such as the Pacific Northwest Aquatic Monitoring Partnership, can help to facilitate the process. Specifically, with respect to predation monitoring, decisions need to be made as to what metrics are necessary to assess status and trends in predation. We present a variety of metrics that are dependent on collecting predators and examining their diets. The metrics we present have been used before, but are labor-intensive and, therefore, costly (Petersen and Ward, 1999). Furthermore, the results of these types of studies are not always easily interpreted by key audiences; a characteristic listed above as being problematic for the success of a monitoring program. Metrics other than those used in this study may be as good or better at communicating the status and trends of the underlying driver behind assessing predation: the mortality of juvenile salmonids from fish predators in the Priest Rapids Project. For instance, survival goals have been established for the study area; perhaps survival metrics could serve as a metric to assess mitigation efforts to reduce predators in the study area. Increases in survival should be an indication of reduced mortality from fish predators. Alternately, various other methods have been used to justify and evaluate efforts to mitigate the effects of predators, including monitoring the movements of tagged predators and prey, measuring growth and fecundity of predators, and modeling how juvenile salmonid mortality varies with predator density, river flow, and other variables (Petersen and Ward, 1999). The formulation of an expert panel can help the PRCC work through the development and justification of metrics used to assess predation of juvenile salmon in the study area. However, valuable information can be derived from assessing the diets of fish predators that can help to directly assess predation of juvenile salmonids and the effects of fish predators on other components of the ecosystem in addition to juvenile salmon.

With respect to the development of a sample frame, the USGS has formulated a sample frame for the PRP using a Generalized Random Tessellation Stratified algorithm (Larsen and others, 2007). This sample frame encompasses both the river channel and upland areas. The sample frame was developed as part of efforts to facilitate the development of a long-term monitoring program for aquatic invasive species and as part of efforts to initiate an integrated status and trends monitoring program for aquatic resources in the Columbia River basin (U.S. Geological Survey; unpub. Data, 2011). The sample frame is available upon request and is slated to be made available through a tool being developed by the Pacific Northwest Aquatic Monitoring Partnership (*http://www.pnamp.org/project/3263*).

Acknowledgments

We thank Conrad Frost and Amy Puls of the USGS and Curt Nelson, Fritz Wichterman, Klint Caillier, and seasonal and permanent staff of the WDFW for their assistance in the field and laboratory. We thank Lucinda Morrow and Lance Campbell of the WDFW aging laboratory. In addition, we want to thank Curt Dotson for contract administration and the members of the Priest Rapids Coordinating Committee for their comments and thoughts on this project. We would also acknowledge John Beeman and Matt Mesa, USGS, and Jeffrey Korth, WDFW, for their input and reviews of this report.

References Cited

Beamesderfer, R.C., and Rieman, B.E., 1991, Abundance and distribution of northern squawfish, walleyes and smallmouth bass in the John Day Reservoir, Columbia River: Transactions of the American Fisheries Society, v. 120, p. 439–447.

Beamesderfer, R.C., Ward, D.L., and Nigro, A.A., 1996, Evaluation of the biological basis for a predator control program on northern squawfish (*Ptychocheilus oregonensis*) in the Columbia and Snake rivers: Canadian Journal of Fisheries and Aquatic Sciences, v. 53, p. 2,898–2,908.

Bickford, S.A. and Skalski, J.R, 2000, Reanalysis and interpretation of 25 years of Snake–Columbia River juvenile salmonid survival studies: North American Journal of Fisheries Management, v. 20, p. 53–68.

Bonar, S.A., Bolding, B.D., and Divens, M., 2000, Standard fish sampling guidelines for Washington State ponds and lakes: Olympia, Wash., Washington Department of Fish and Wildlife, Report No. FPT 00-28.

Brandt, S.B., and Hartman, K.J., 1993, Innovative approaches with bioenergetics models—Future applications to fish ecology and management: Transactions of the American Fisheries Society, v. 122, p. 731–735.

Burley C.C., and Poe, T.P, 1994, Significance of predation in the Columbia River from Priest Rapids Dam to Chief Joseph Dam: Prepared for Chelan, Douglas, and Grant County Public Utility Districts, Washington, by Washington Department of Wildlife and National Biological Survey, Olympia, Wash.

Cech, J.J., Jr., Castleberry, D.T., Hopkins, T.E., and Petersen, J.H., 1994, Northern squawfish, *Ptychocheilus oregonensis,* Ch consumption rate and respiration model—Effects of temperature and body size: Canadian Journal of Fisheries and Aquatic Sciences, v. 51, p. 8–12.

Cochran, W.G., 1977, Sampling techniques (3d ed.): New York, Wiley.

Counihan, T.D., Miller, A.I., and Parsley, M.J., 1999: Indexing the relative abundance of age–0 white sturgeons in an impoundment of the lower Columbia River from highly skewed trawling data: North American Journal of Fisheries Management, v. 19, p. 520–529.

Coutant, C.C., and Whitney, R.R., 2000: Fish behavior in relation to passage through hydropower turbines—A review: Transactions of the American Fisheries Society, v. 129, p. 351–380.

Cummins, K.W., and Wuycheck, J.C., 1971, Caloric equivalents for investigations in ecological energetics: Mitteilungen International Vereinigung für Theoretische und Angewandte Limnologie, v. 18, p. 1–151.

Dieterman, D.J., Thorn, W.C., and Anderson, C.S., 2004: Application of a bioenergetics model for brown trout to evaluate growth in southeast Minnesota streams: Minnesota Department of Natural Resources Policy Section, Fisheries and Wildlife Investigational Report 513.

Donabauer, S.B., 2010, Comparing otoliths, dorsal spines and scales to estimate age, growth, and mortality between male and female walleye from Brookville reservoir, Indiana: Final Report, Fisheries Section, Indiana Department of Natural Resources, Indiana Division of Fish and Wildlife.

Erickson, C.M., 1983: Age determination of Manitoban walleye using otoliths, dorsal spines, and scales: North American Journal of Fisheries Management, v. 3, p. 176–181.

Federal Energy Regulatory Commission, 2008, Priest Rapids Project license agreement: Federal Energy Regulatory Commission, accessed June 5, 2012, at *http://www.gcpud.org/pudDocuments/naturalResourcesDocs/h1.pdf.*

Garner, K., and Keeler, C., 2008, Northern Pikeminnow (*Ptychocheilus oregonensis*) removal efforts for the Priest Rapids Project, mid-Columbia River, 2008: Priest Rapids Hydroelectric Project (FERC No. 2114) Public Utility District No. 2 of Grant County, P.O. Box 878, Ephrata, Wash.

Garner, K., and Keeler, C., 2009: Northern Pikeminnow (*Ptychocheilus oregonensis*) removal efforts for the Priest Rapids Project, mid-Columbia River, 2009: Priest Rapids Hydroelectric Project (FERC No. 2114) Public Utility District No .2 of Grant County, P.O. Box 878, Ephrata, Wash.

Hanchin, P.A., 2011, The fish community and fishery of Lake Gogebic, Gogebic and Ontonagon Counties, Michigan in 2005–06 with emphasis on Walleye, Northern Pike, and Smallmouth Bass: Michigan Department of Natural Resources, Fisheries Division, Fisheries Special Report 58.

Hanson, P.C., Johnson, T.B., Schindler, D.E., and Kitchell, J.F., 1997, Bioenergetics Model 3.0 for Windows: Madison, Wis., University of Wisconsin Sea Grant Institute, Technical Report WISCUT-T-97-001.

Hardiman, J.M., Counihan, T.D., Burgess, D.S., Simmons, K.E., Holmberg, G., Rogala, J.A., and Polacek, R.R., 2012, Assessing fish predation on migrating juvenile steelhead and a retrospective comparison to steelhead survival through the Priest Rapids Hydroelectric Project, Columbia River, Washington, 2009–11: U.S. Geological Survey Open-File Report 2012–1129, 36 p.

Harmon, J.R., and Parks D.L., 1980, Evaluation of a bypass system for juvenile salmonids at Little Goose Dam: Marine Fisheries Review, v. 42, p. 25–28.

Isermann, D.A., Meerbeek, J. R., Scholten, G.D., and Willis, D.W., 2003. Evaluation of three different structures used for walleye age estimation with emphasis on removal and processing times. North American Journal of Fisheries Management 23:625–631.

Iwamato, R.N., Muir, W.D., Sandford, McIntyre, Frost, D.A., Williams, J.G., Smith, S.G., and Skalski, J.R., 1994, Survival estimates for the passage of juvenile Chinook salmon through Snake River dams and reservoirs, 1993:. Report prepared for the U.S. Department of Energy, Bonneville Power Administration Division of Fish and Wildlife, Contract DE-A179-93BP10891, Project 93-29, 139 p.

Jearld, A., Jr. 1983, Age determination, *in* Nielsen, L.A., and Johnson, D.L., eds, Fisheries techniques: Bethesda, Md., American Fisheries Society.

Johnson, G.E., Anglea, S.M., Adams, N.S., and Wik, T.O., 2005, Evaluation of a prototype surface flow bypass for juvenile salmon and steelhead at the powerhouse of Lower Granite Dam, Snake River, Washington, 1996–2000: North American Journal of Fisheries Management, v. 25, p. 138–151.

Larsen, D.P., Olsen, A.R., and Stevens, D.L., 2007, Using a master sample to integrate stream monitoring programs: Journal of Agricultural, Biological, and Environmental Statistics, v. 13, no. 3, p. 243–254, doi:10.1198/108571108X336593.

Knutsen, C.J., and Ward, D.L., 1999, Biological characteristics of northern pikeminnow in the lower Columbia and Snake Rivers before and after sustained exploitation: Transactions of the American Fisheries Society, v. 128, p. 1,008–1,019.

Larsen, D.P., Olsen, A.R., Lanigan, S.H., Moyer, C., Jones, K.K., and Kincaid, T.M., 2007, Sound survey designs can facilitate integrating stream monitoring data across multiple programs: Journal of the American Water Resources Association, v. 43, p. 384–397.

Le Cren, E.D., 1947, The determination of the age and growth of the perch (*Perca fluviatilis*) from the opercular bone: The Journal of Animal Ecology, v. 16, p. 188–204.

Mateo, I., 2007, A bioenergetics based comparison of growth conversion efficiency of Atlantic cod on Georges Bank and in the Gulf of Main: Journal of Northwest Atlantic Fisheries Science, v. 38, p. 23–35.

McCarthy, S.G., Duda, J.J., Emlen, J.M., Hodgson, G.R., and Beauchamp., D.A., 2009, Linking habitat quality with trophic performance of steelhead along forest gradients in the south fork Trinity River watershed, California: Transactions of the American Fisheries Society, v. 138 p. 506–521.

Muir, W.D., Smith, S.G., Iwamoto, R.N., Kamikawa, D.J., McIntyre, K.W., Hockersmith, E.E., Sandford, B.P., Ocker, P.A., Ruehle, T.E., and Williams, J.G., 1995, Survival estimates for the passage of juvenile salmonids through Snake River Dams and reservoirs, 1994: Annual report prepared for the Bonneville Power Administration, Portland, Oreg., and U.S. Army Corps of Engineers, Walla Walla, Wash., Contract DE93-29A179-93B101891, Project 93-29, 187 p.

National Marine Fisheries Service, 2004, Biological Opinion and Magnuson-Steven Fishery Conservation and Management Act Interim Protection Plan for Operation of the Priest Rapids Hydroelectric Project, May 3, 2004: National Marine Fisheries Service, 115 p..

National Marine Fisheries Service, 2008, Biological Opinion and Magnuson-Steven Fishery Conservation and Management Act New License for the Priest Rapids Hydroelectric Projec, February 1, 2008: National Marine Fisheries Service, 74 p..

Naughton,G.P., Bennett, D.H., and Newman, B., 2004, Predation on juvenile salmonids by smallmouth bass in the Lower Granite reservoir system, Snake River: North American Journal of Fisheries Management, v. 24, no. 2, p. 534–544.

Petersen, J.H., and Ward, D.L. 1999, Development and corroboration of a bioenergetics model for northern pikeminnow (*Ptychocheilus oregonensis*) feeding on juvenile salmonids in the Columbia River: Transactions of the American Fisheries Society, v. 128, p. 784–801.

Petersen, J.H., 1994, Importance of spatial pattern in estimating predation on juvenile salmonids in the Columbia River: Transactions of the American Fisheries Society, v. 123, p. 924–930.

Petersen, J.H., 2002, Compensatory feeding following a predator removal program—Detection and mechanisms: Reports to Bonneville Power Administration, Contract No. 0003395, Project No. 199007800, BPA report DOE/BP-00003395-1, 92 electronic p..

Pfeifer, B., Hagen, J.E., Weitkamp, D., Bennett, D.H., Lukas, J., and Dresser, T., 2001, Evaluation of fish species present in the Priest Rapids Project area, mid-Columbia River, Washington, USA: Prepared for Public Utility District No. 2 of Grant County, Ephrata, Wash.

Ransom, B.H., and Steig, T.W., 1995, Comparison of the effectiveness of surface flow and deep spill for bypassing Pacific salmon smolts (*Onhorhynchus spp.*) at Columbia River Basin hydropower dams: San Francisco, Calif., Proceedings of the International Conference on Hydropower, Waterpower 1995, July 25–28.

Raymond, H.L., 1979, Effects of dams and impounds on migrations of juvenile Chinook salmon and steelhead from the Snake River, 1966 to 1975: Transactions of the American Fisheries Society, v. 108, p. 505–529.

Rieman B., Beamesderfer, R., Vigg, S., and Poe, T, 1991, Estimated loss of juvenile salmonids to predation by northern squawfish, walleyes, and smallmouth bass in John Day Reservoir, Columbia River: Transactions of the American Fisheries Society, v. 120, p. 448–458.

Robichaud, D., Nass, B., Timko, M.A., English, K.K., and Ransom, B., 2005: Analysis of Chinook smolt behavior and relative survival at Wanapum Dam using three-dimensional acoustic telemetry, 2004: Report for Public Utility District No. 2 of Grant County, Ephrata, Wash.

Rogers, J.B., and Burley, C.C., 1991, A sigmoid model to predict gastric evacuation rates of smallmouth bass (*Micropterus dolomieui*) fed juvenile salmon: Canadian Journal of Fisheries and Aquatic Sciences, v. 48, p. 933–937.

Rogers, M.W., Hansen, M.J., and Beard, T.D., 2003, Catchability of walleyes to fyke netting and electrofishing in northern Wisconsin lakes: North American Journal of Fisheries Management, v. 23, issue 4, p. 1,193–1,206.

Schoenebeck, C.W., and Hansen, M.J., 2005, Electrofishing catchability of walleyes, largemouth bass, smallmouth bass, northern pike, and muskellunge in Wisconsin lakes: North American Journal of Fisheries Management, v. 25, issue 4, p. 1,341–1,352.

Stewart, D.J., Weininger, D., Rottiers, D.V., and Edsall, T.A., 1983, An energetics model for lake trout, *Salvelinus namaycush*—Application to the Lake Michigan population: Canadian Journal of Fisheries and Aquatic Sciences, v. 40, p. 681–698.

Stier, D.J., and Kynard, B., 1986, Use of radio telemetry to determine the mortality of Atlantic salmon smolts passed through a 17-MW Kaplan turbine at a low-head hydroelectric dam: Transactions of the American Fisheries Society, v. 115, p. 771–775.

Sullivan, B.E., Prahl, F.G., Small, L.F., and Covert, P.A., 2001, Seasonality of phytoplankton production in the Columbia River—A natural or anthropogenic pattern?: Geochimica et Cosmochimica Acta, v. 65, no. 7, p. 1,125–1,139.

Timko, M.A., Brown, L.S., Wright, C.D., O'Connor, R.R., Fitzgerald, C.A., Meager, M.L., Rizor, S.E., Nealson, P.A., and Johnston, S.V., 2007a, Analysis of juvenile Chinook, steelhead, and sockeye salmon behavior using acoustic tags at Wanapum and Priest Rapids Dams, 2006: Draft report by HTI, Seattle, Wash., for Public Utility District No. 2 of Grant County, Ephrata, Wash.

Timko, M.A., Sullivan, L.S., Wright, C.D., Rizor, S.E., Fitzgerald, C.A., O'Connor, R.R., and Meager, M.L., 2007b, Analysis of juvenile Chinook, steelhead and sockeye salmon behavior using acoustic tags at Wanapum and Priest Rapids dams, 2007: Draft report by HTI, Seattle, Wash., for Public Utility District No. 2 of Grant County, Ephrata, Wash.

University of Washington, 2012, Columbia River data access in real time (DART): Seattle, Wash., University of Washington School of Aquatic and Fishery Science Web site, accessed June 1, 2012, at *http://www.cbr.washington.edu/dart/*.

U.S. Fish and Wildlife Service, National Marine Fisheries Service, Washington Department of Fish and Wildlife, Confederated Tribes of the Colville Reservation, and Yakama Nation, 2006, Settlement Agreement entered into by Public Utility District No. 2 of Grant County, Wash.: U.S. Fish and Wildlife Service, National Marine Fisheries Service, Washington Department of Fish and Wildlife, Confederated Tribes of the Colville Reservation, and Yakama Nation.

Vigg S., Poe, T.P., Prendergast, L.A., and Hansel, H.C., 1991, Rates of consumption of juvenile salmonids and alternative prey fish by northern squawfish, walleyes, smallmouth bass and channel catfish in John Day Reservoir, Columbia River: Transactions of the American Fisheries Society, v. 120, p. 421438.

Ward D.L., Petersen, J.H., and Loch, J.J., 1995, Index of predation on juvenile salmonids by northern squawfish in the lower and middle Columbia River and in the lower Snake River: Transactions of the American Fisheries Society, v. 124, p. 321–334.

Ward, D.L., and Zimmerman, M.P., 1999, Response of smallmouth bass to sustained removals of northern pikeminnow in the lower Columbia and Snake Rivers: Transactions of the American Fisheries Society, v. 128 p. 1,020–1,035.

Windell, J.T., 1978, Estimating food consumption rates of fish populations, *in* Bagenal, T., ed., Methods for assessment of fish production in fresh waters: London, Blackwell Scientific Publications, p. 227–254.

Zimmerman, M.P., 1999, Food habits of smallmouth bass, walleyes, and northern pikeminnow in the lower Columbia River basin during outmigration of juvenile anadromous salmonids: Transactions of the American Fisheries Society, v. 128, p. 1,036–1,054.

Zimmerman, M.P., and Ward, D.L., 1999, Index of predation on juvenile salmonids by northern pikeminnow in the lower Columbia River Basin, 1994–1996: Transactions of the American Fisheries Society, v. 128, no. 6, p. 995–1,007.

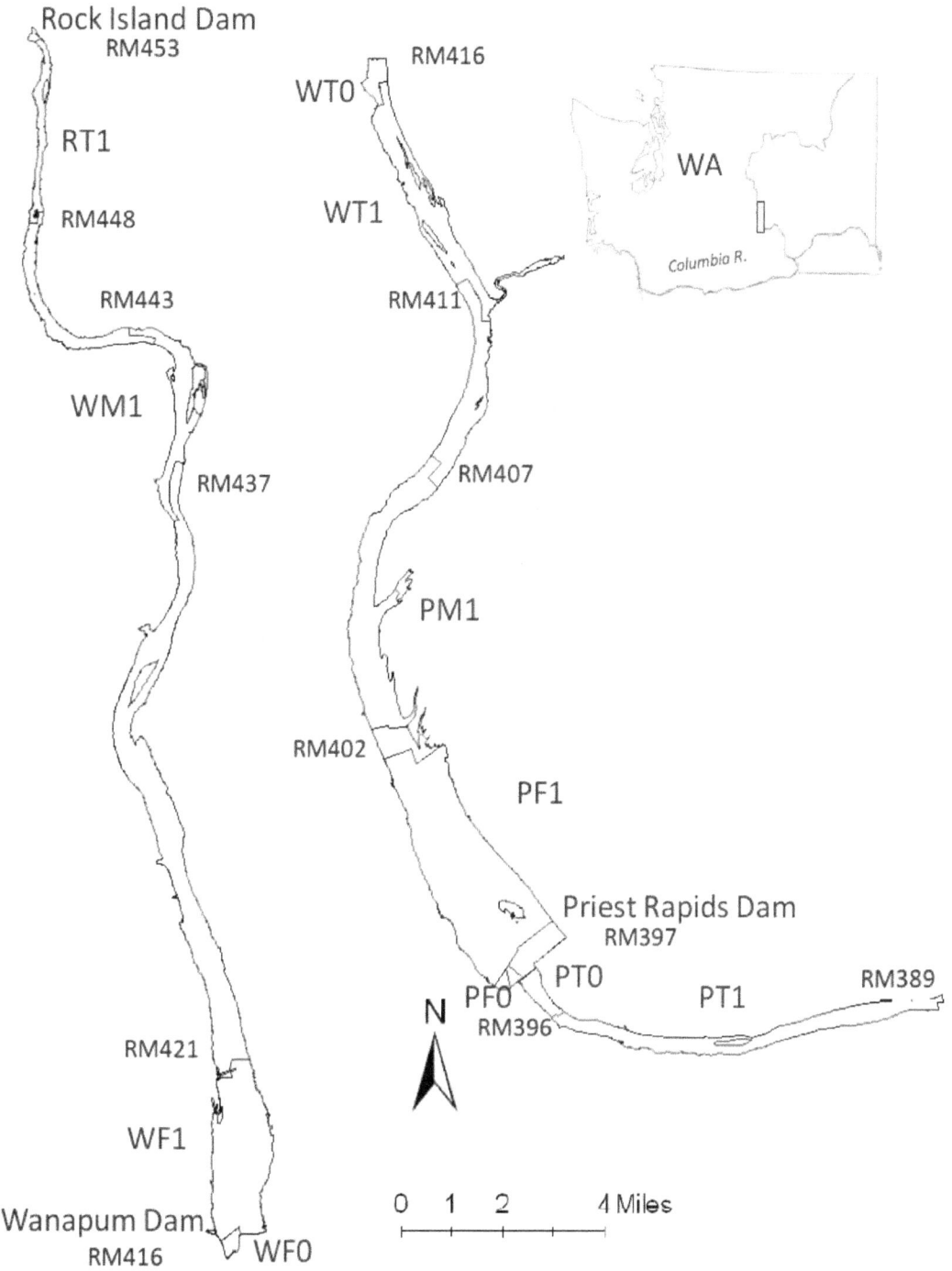

Figure 1. Study area sampled in the Columbia River, Washington, 2009. Reach locations: PT1, Priest Rapids Tailrace; PT0, Priest Rapids Tailrace BRZ; PF0, Priest Rapids Forebay BRZ; PF1, Priest Rapids Forebay; PM1, Priest Rapids Mid-Reservoir; WT1, Wanapum Tailrace; WT0, Wanapum Tailrace BRZ; WF0, Wanapum Forebay BRZ; WF1, Wanapum Forebay; WM1, Wanapum Mid-Reservoir; RT1, Rock Island Tailrace. RM, river mile.

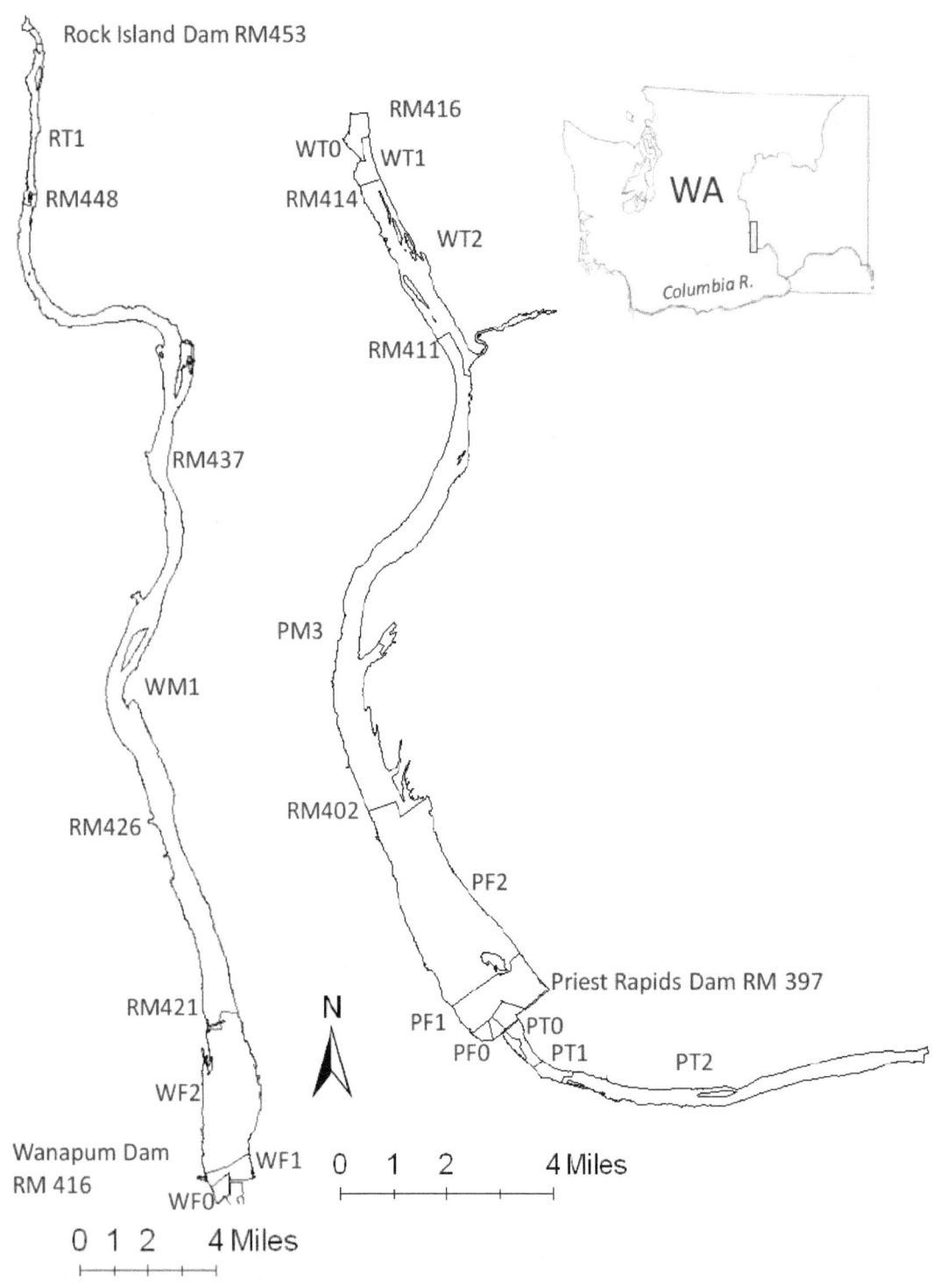

Figure 2. Study area sampled in the Columbia River, Washington, 2010. Reach locations: PT1, Priest Rapids Tailrace; PT0, Priest Rapids Tailrace BRZ; PF0, Priest Rapids Forebay BRZ; PF1, Priest Rapids Forebay; PM1, Priest Rapids Mid-Reservoir; WT1, Wanapum Tailrace; WT0, Wanapum Tailrace BRZ; WF0, Wanapum Forebay BRZ; WF1, Wanapum Forebay; WM1, Wanapum Mid-Reservoir; RT1, Rock Island Tailrace. RM, river mile.

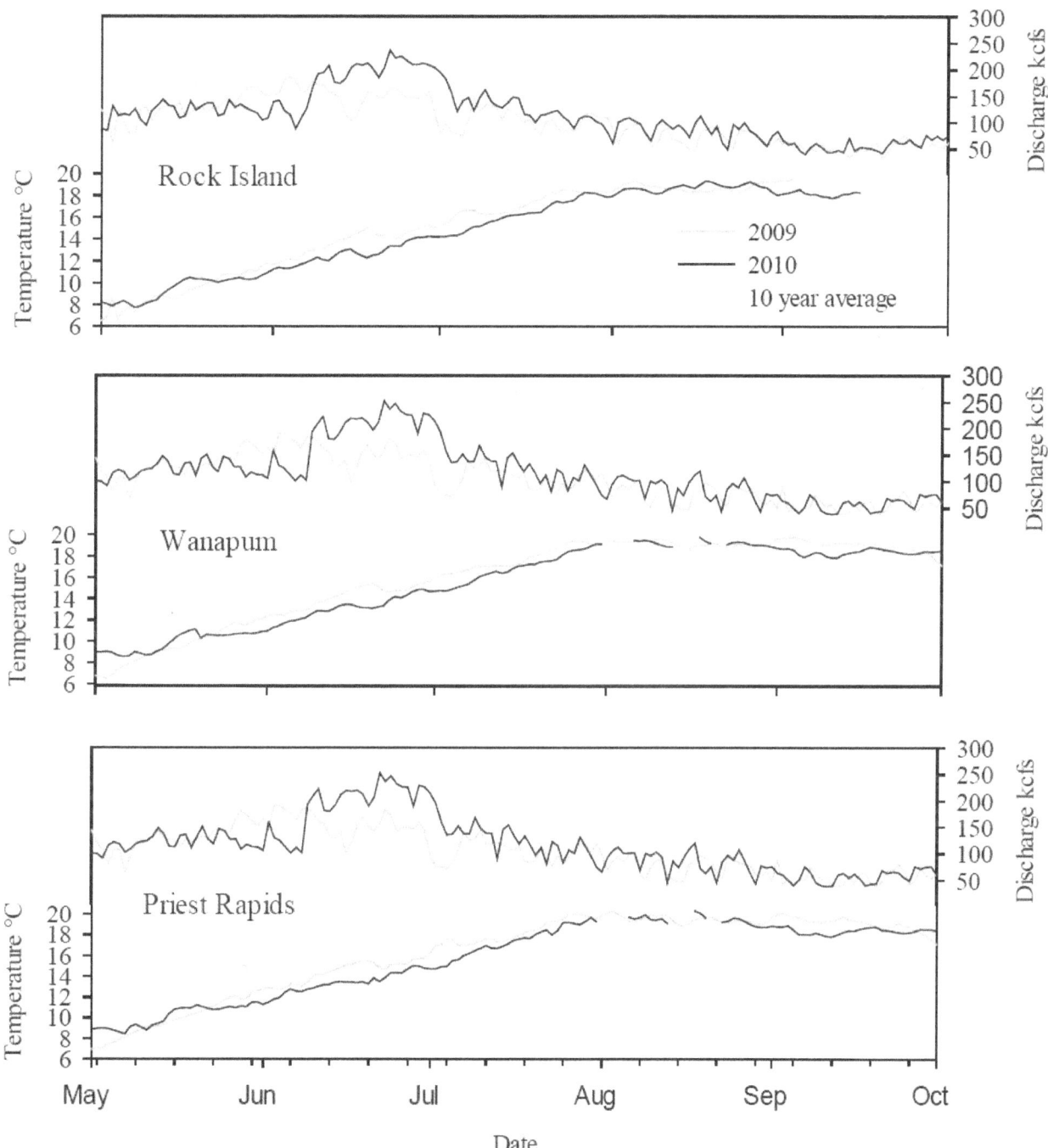

Figure 3. River discharge (1,000 cubic feet second) and water temperature as measured in the tailrace of Priest Rapids, Wanapum, and Rock Island Dams, Columbia River, Washington, from May to October. Discharge data from tailrace outflow. Temperature data from the Water Quality Meter station, downloaded from the University of Washington Columbia River Data access in real time Web site.

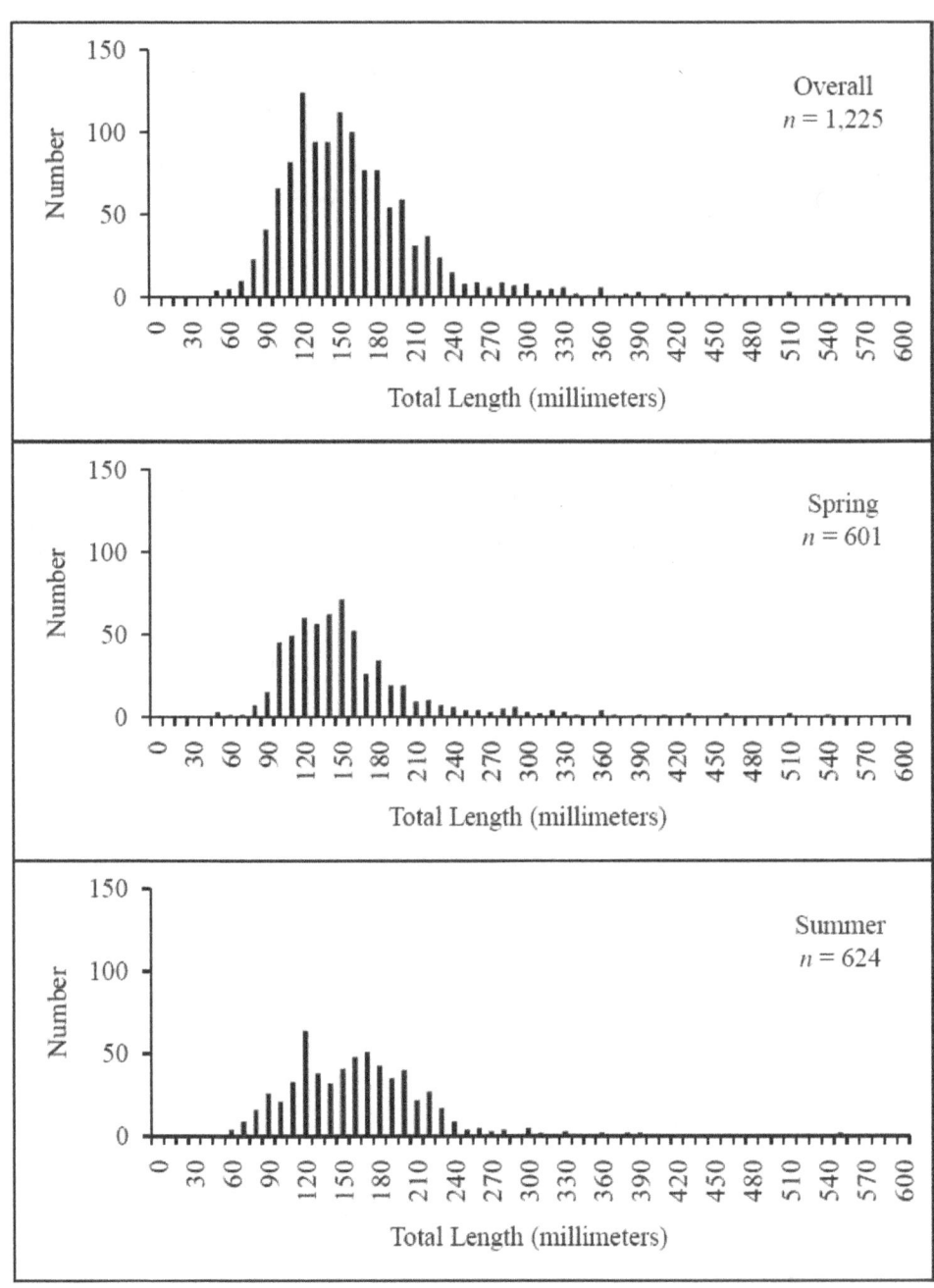

Figure 4. Length frequency histograms for northern pikeminnow during Burley and Poe sampling overall in 2009 (May 27–June 12 and August 3–20), in spring 2009 (May 27–June 12), and in summer 2009 (August 3–20), Priest Rapids Project, Columbia River, Washington. *n*, total number of fish.

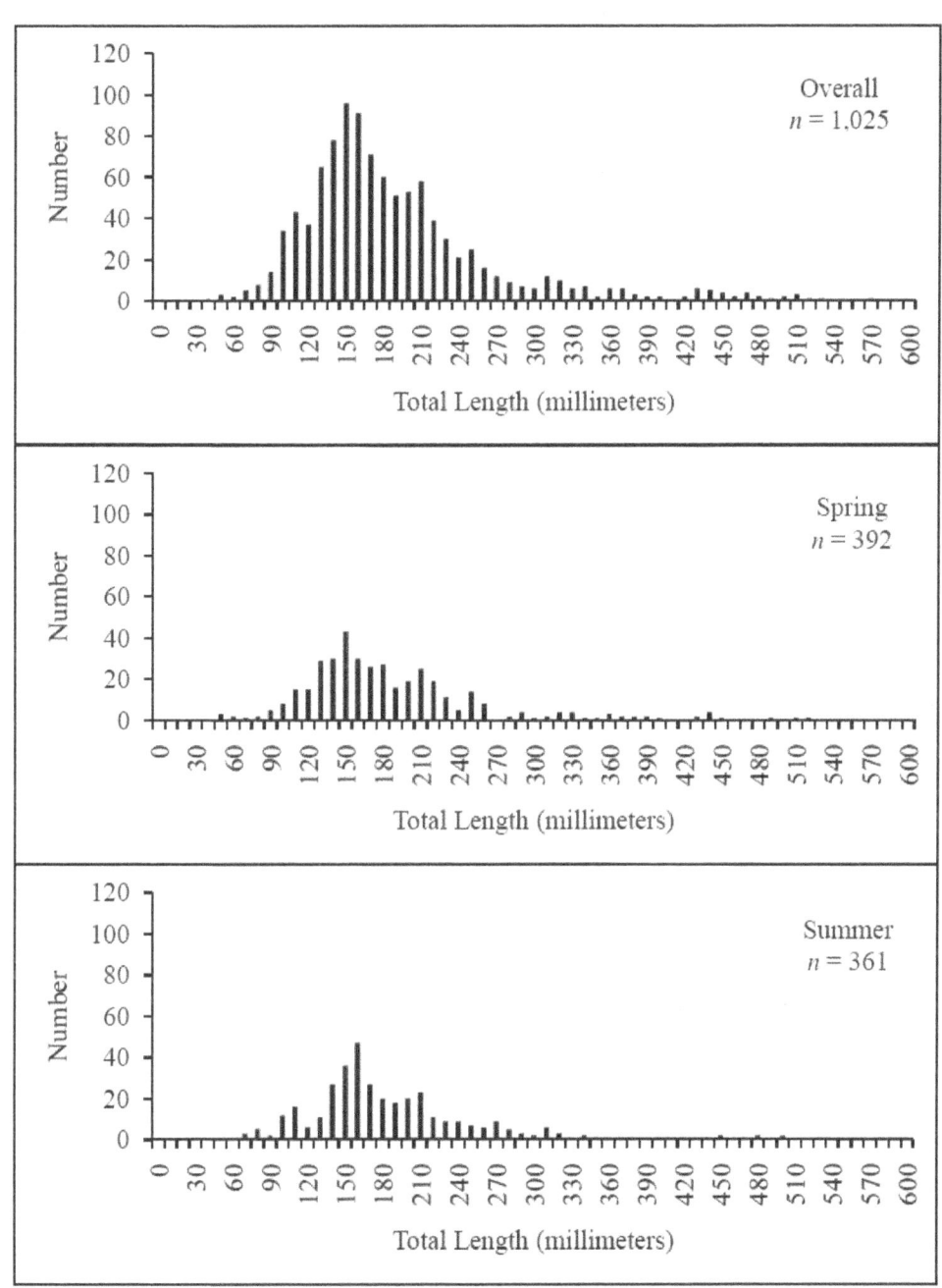

Figure 5. Length frequency histograms for northern pikeminnow during predator index sampling overall in 2009 (May 1–August 27), in spring 2009 (May 7–June 11), and in summer 2009 (June 23–August 5), Priest Rapids Project, Columbia River, Washington. *n*, total number of fish.

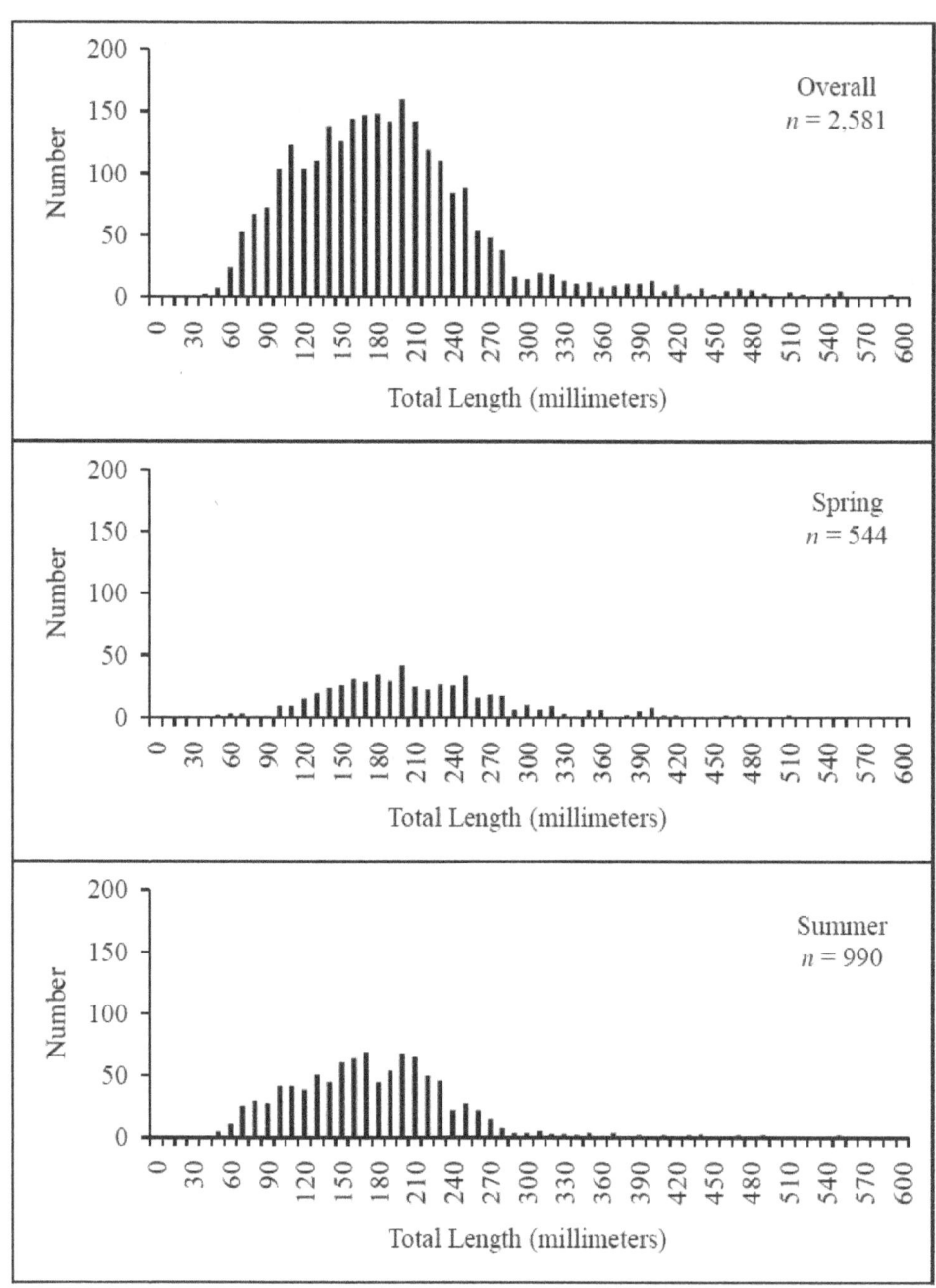

Figure 6. Length frequency histograms for northern pikeminnow during predator index sampling overall in 2010 (May 19–September 3), in spring 2010 (May 19–June 8), and in summer 2010 (June 28–August 11), Priest Rapids Project, Columbia River, Washington. *n*, total number of fish.

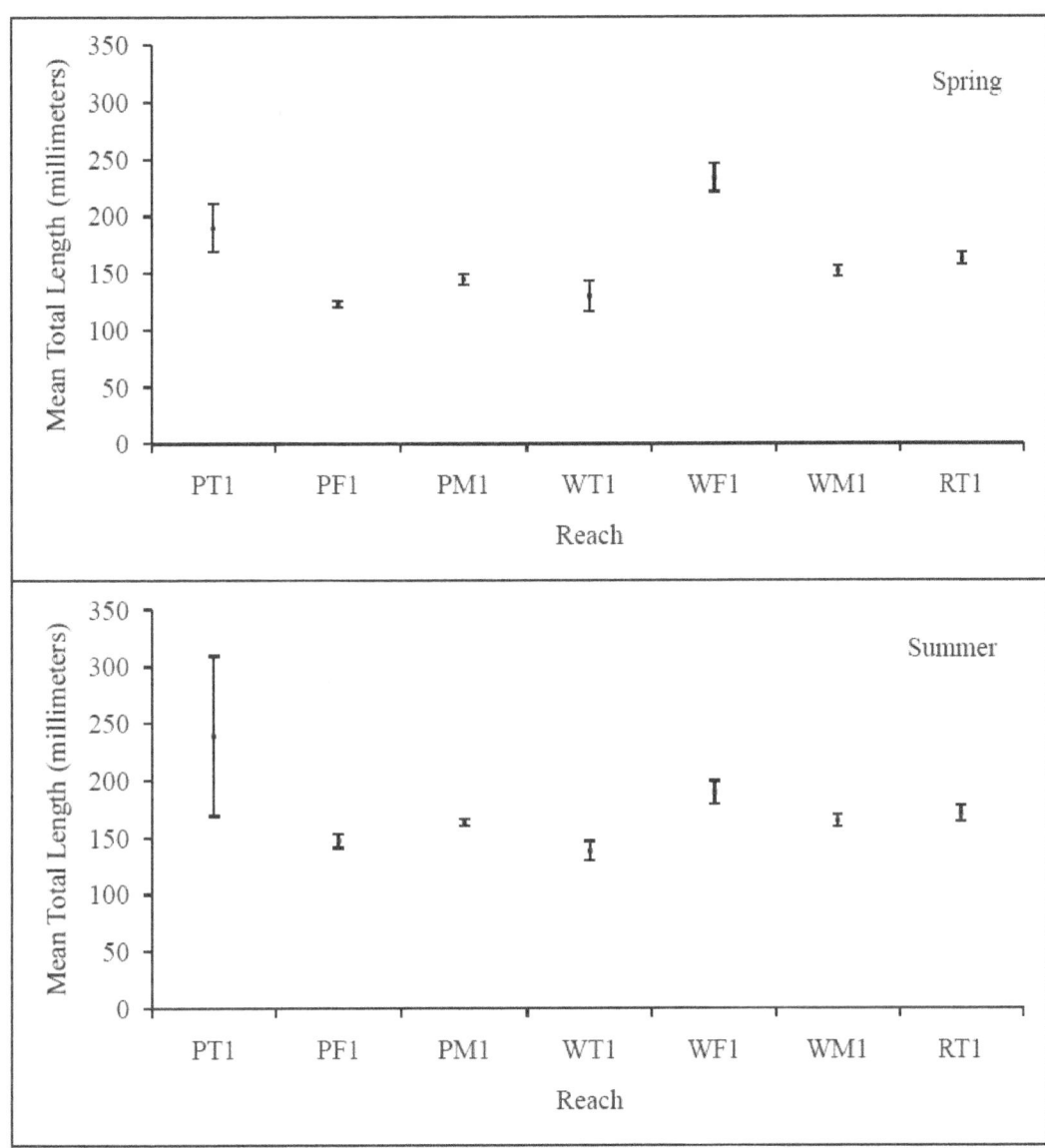

Figure 7. Mean length and one standard error for northern pikeminnow during Burley and Poe sampling in spring 2009 (May 27–June 12) and summer 2009 (August 3–20), by reaches, Priest Rapids Project, Columbia River, Washington. Reach locations: PT1, Priest Rapids Tailrace; PF1, Priest Rapids Forebay; PM1, Priest Rapids Mid-Reservoir; WT1, Wanapum Tailrace; WF1, Wanapum Forebay; WM1, Wanapum Mid-Reservoir; RT1, Rock Island Tailrace.

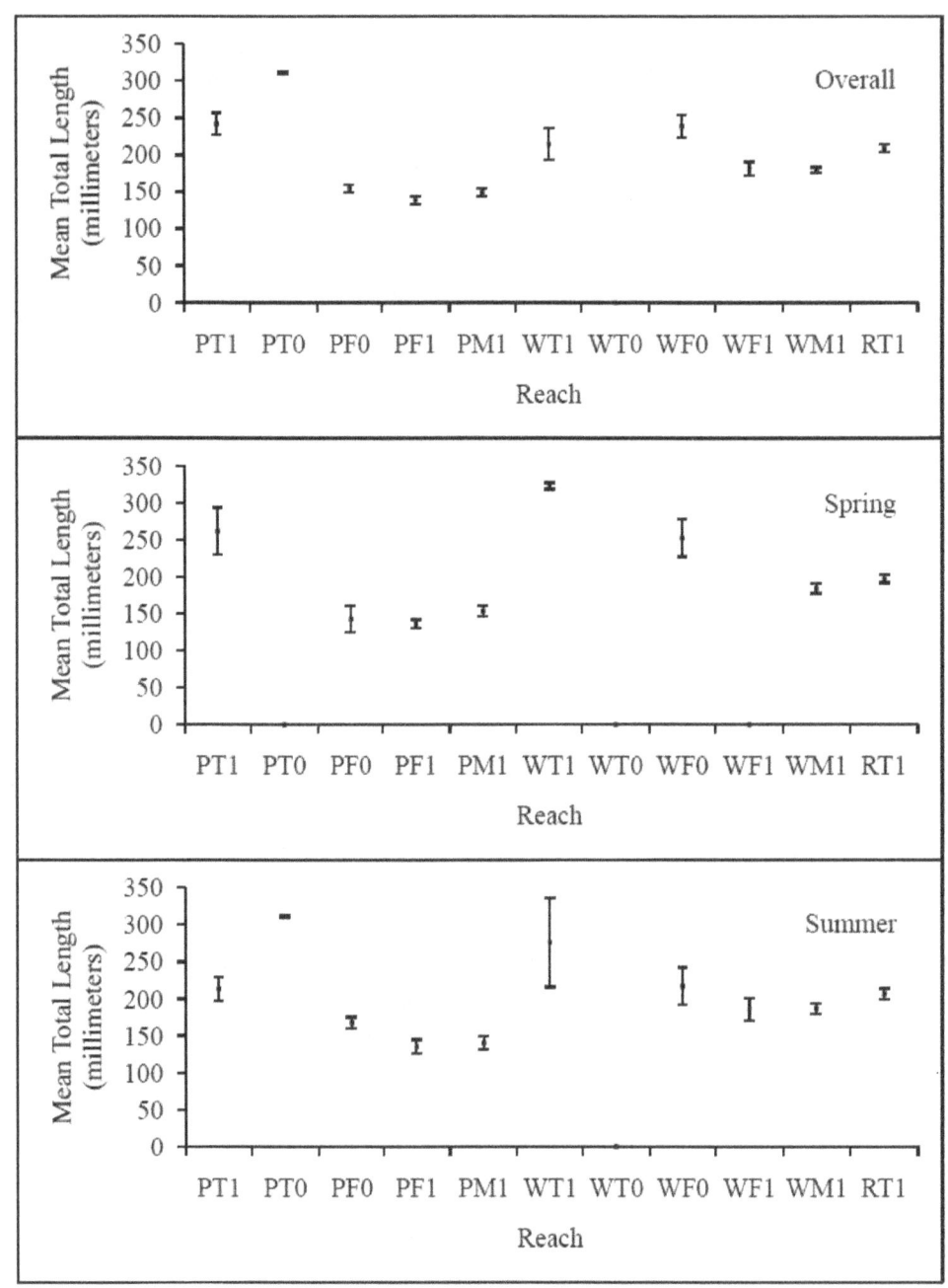

Figure 8. Mean length and one standard error for northern pikeminnow during predator index sampling overall in 2009 (May 1–August 27), in spring 2009 (May 7–June 11), and in summer 2009 (June 23–August 5), by reaches, Priest Rapids Project, Columbia River, Washington. Reach locations: PT1, Priest Rapids Tailrace; PT0, Priest Rapids Tailrace BRZ; PF0, Priest Rapids Forebay BRZ; PF1, Priest Rapids Forebay; PM1, Priest Rapids Mid-Reservoir; WT1, Wanapum Tailrace; WT0, Wanapum Tailrace BRZ; WF0, Wanapum Forebay BRZ; WF1, Wanapum Forebay; WM1, Wanapum Mid-Reservoir; RT1, Rock Island Tailrace.

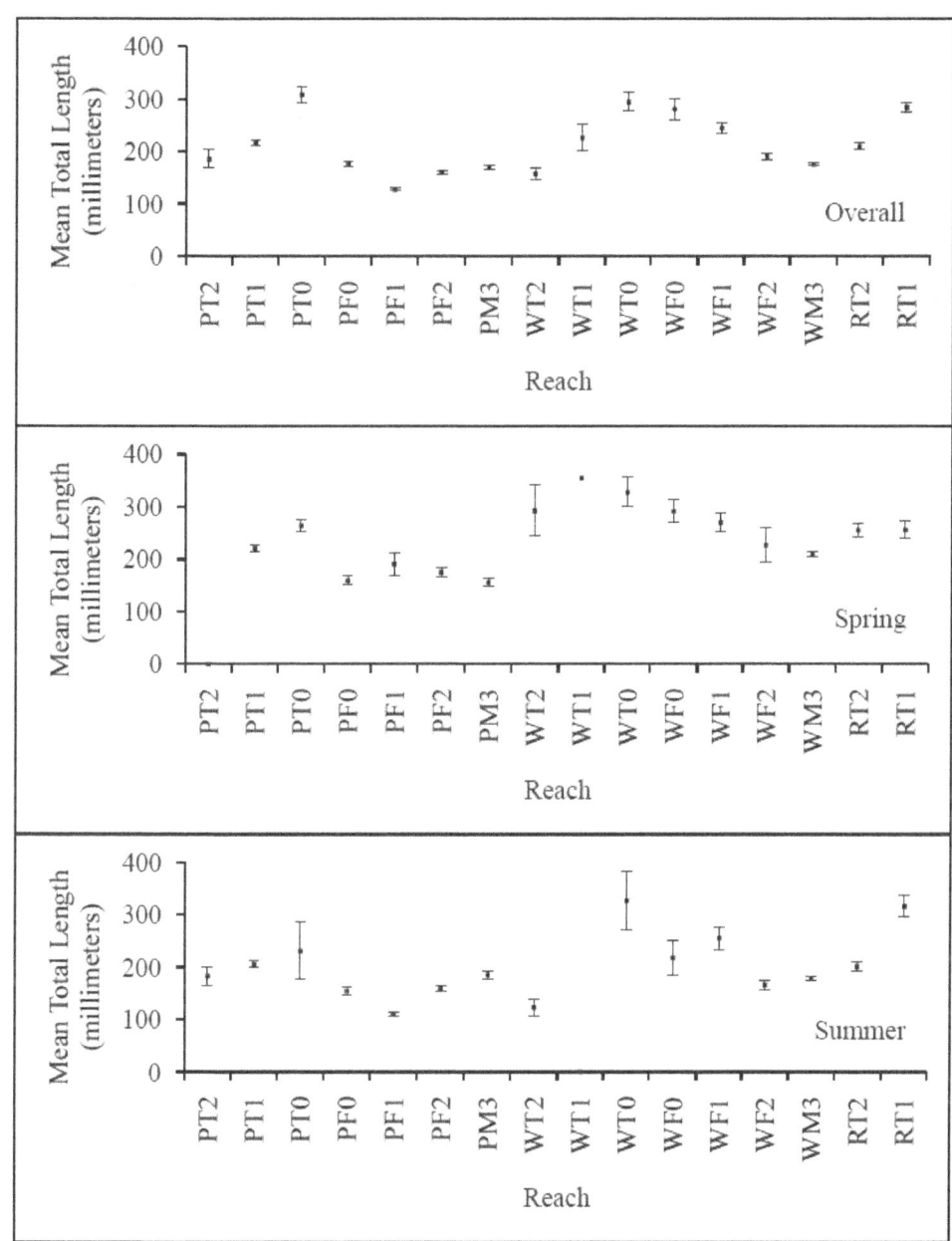

Figure 9. Mean length and one standard error for northern pikeminnow during predator index sampling overall in 2010 (May 19–September 3), in spring 2010 (May 19–June 8), and in summer 2010 (June 28–August 11), by reaches, Priest Rapids Project, Columbia River, Washington. Reach locations: PT2, Priest Rapids Tailrace; PT1, Priest Rapids Tailrace near-BRZ; PT0, Priest Rapids Tailrace BRZ; PF0, Priest Rapids Forebay BRZ; PF1, Priest Rapids Forebay near-BRZ; PF2, Priest Rapids Forebay; PM3, Priest Rapids Mid-Reservoir; WT2, Wanapum Tailrace; WT1, Wanapum Tailrace near-BRZ; WT0, Wanapum Tailrace BRZ; WF0, Wanapum Forebay BRZ; WF1, Wanapum Forebay near-BRZ; WF2, Wanapum Forebay; WM3, Wanapum Mid-Reservoir; RT2, Rock Island Tailrace; RT1, Rock Island Tailrace near-BRZ.

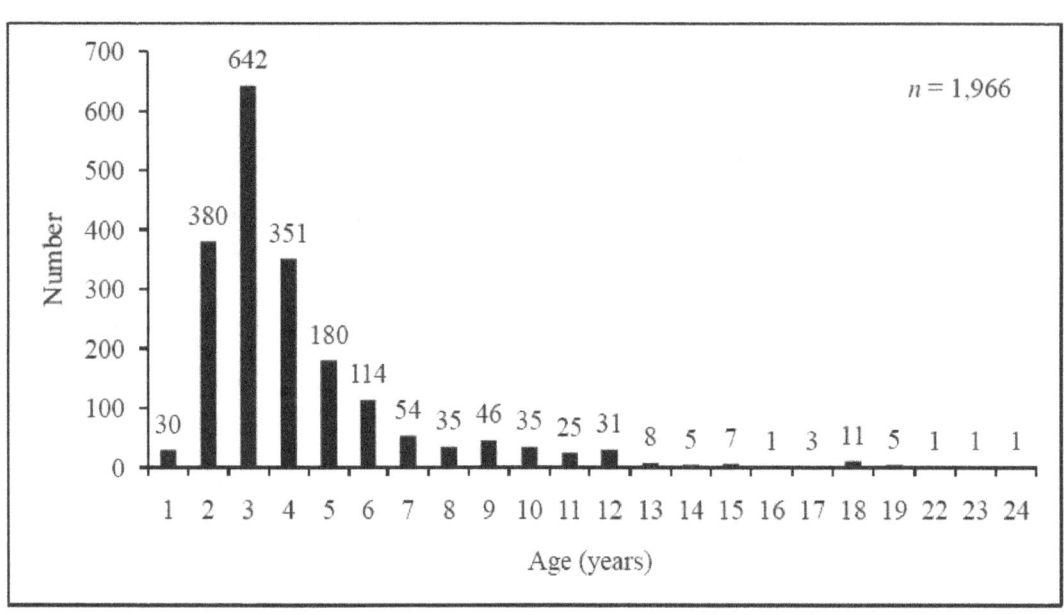

Figure 10. Age frequency (number) of northern pikeminnow captured, Priest Rapids Project, Columbia River, Washington, 2009–11. *n*, total number of fish.

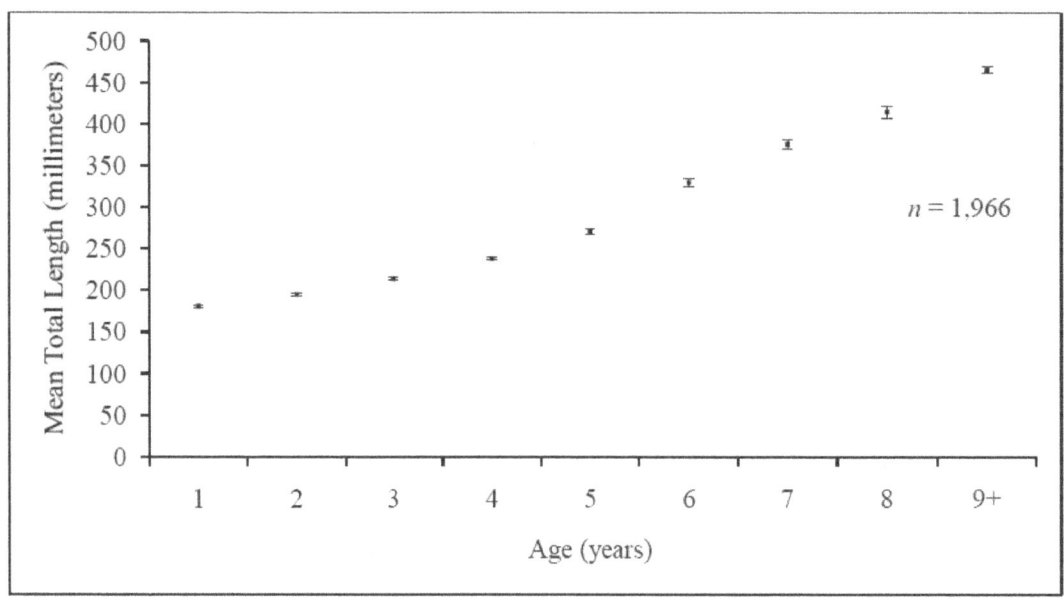

Figure 11. Mean length at age and one standard error for northern pikeminnow captured, Priest Rapids Project, Columbia River, Washington, 2009–11. Fish 9 years old and older are combined. *n*, total number of fish.

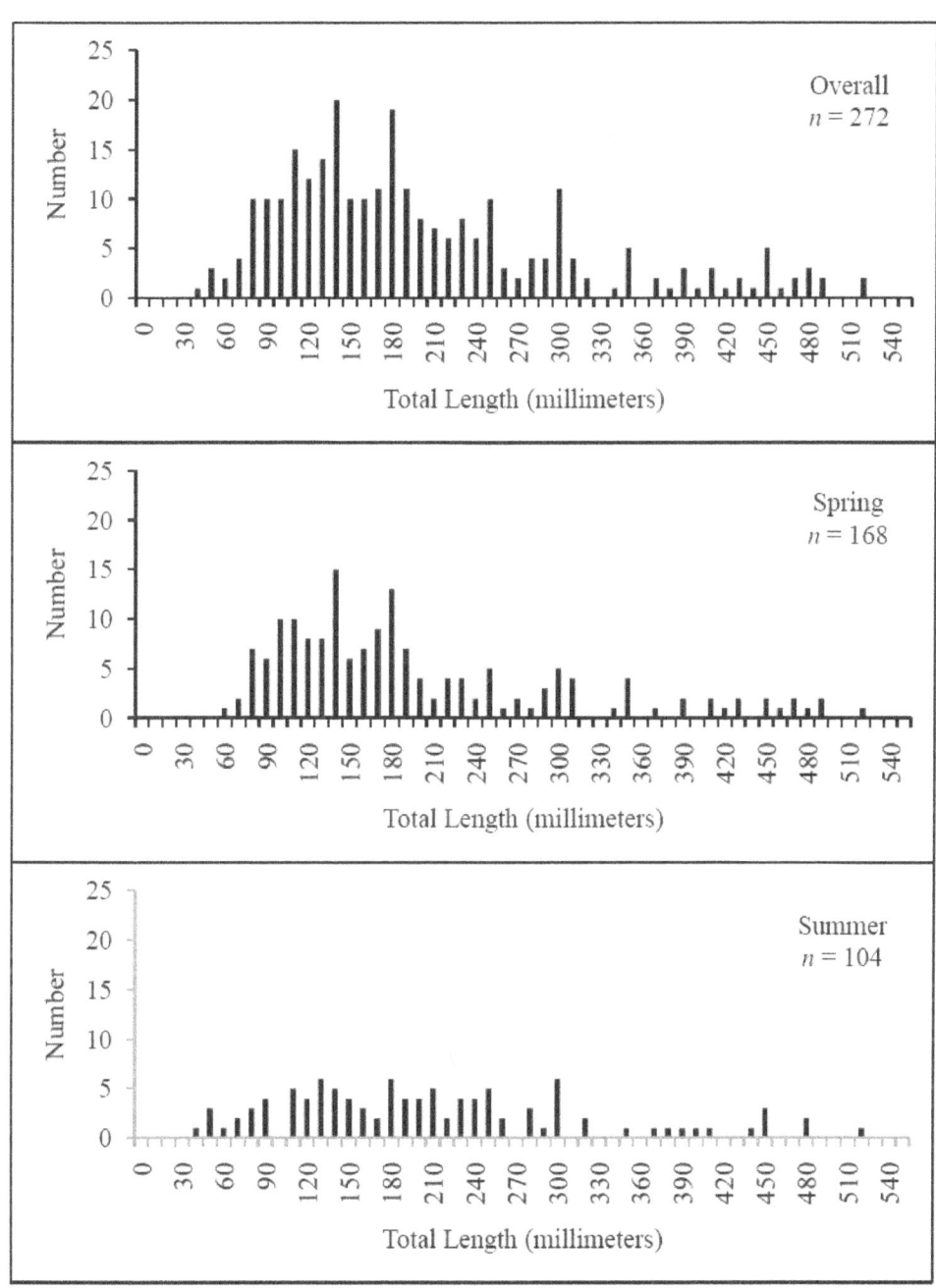

Figure 12. Length frequency histograms for smallmouth bass during Burley and Poe sampling overall in 2009 (May 27–June 12 and August 3–20), in spring 2009 (May 27–June 12), and in summer 2009 (August 3–20), Priest Rapids Project, Columbia River, Washington. *n*, total number of fish.

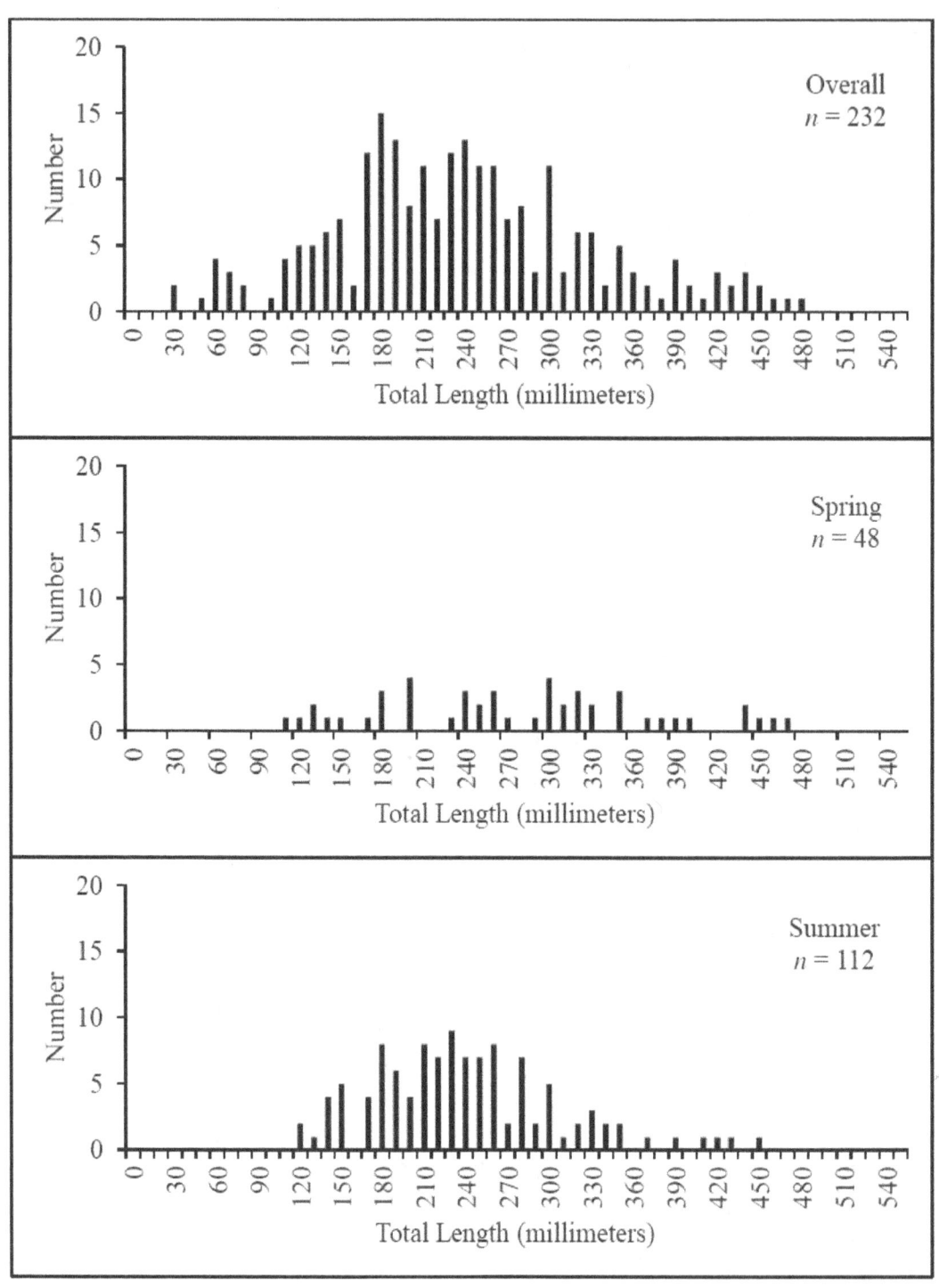

Figure 13. Length frequency histograms for smallmouth bass during predator index sampling overall in 2009 (May 1–August 27), in spring 2009 (May 7–June 11) and in summer 2009 (June 23–August 5), Priest Rapids Project, Columbia River, Washington. *n*, total number of fish.

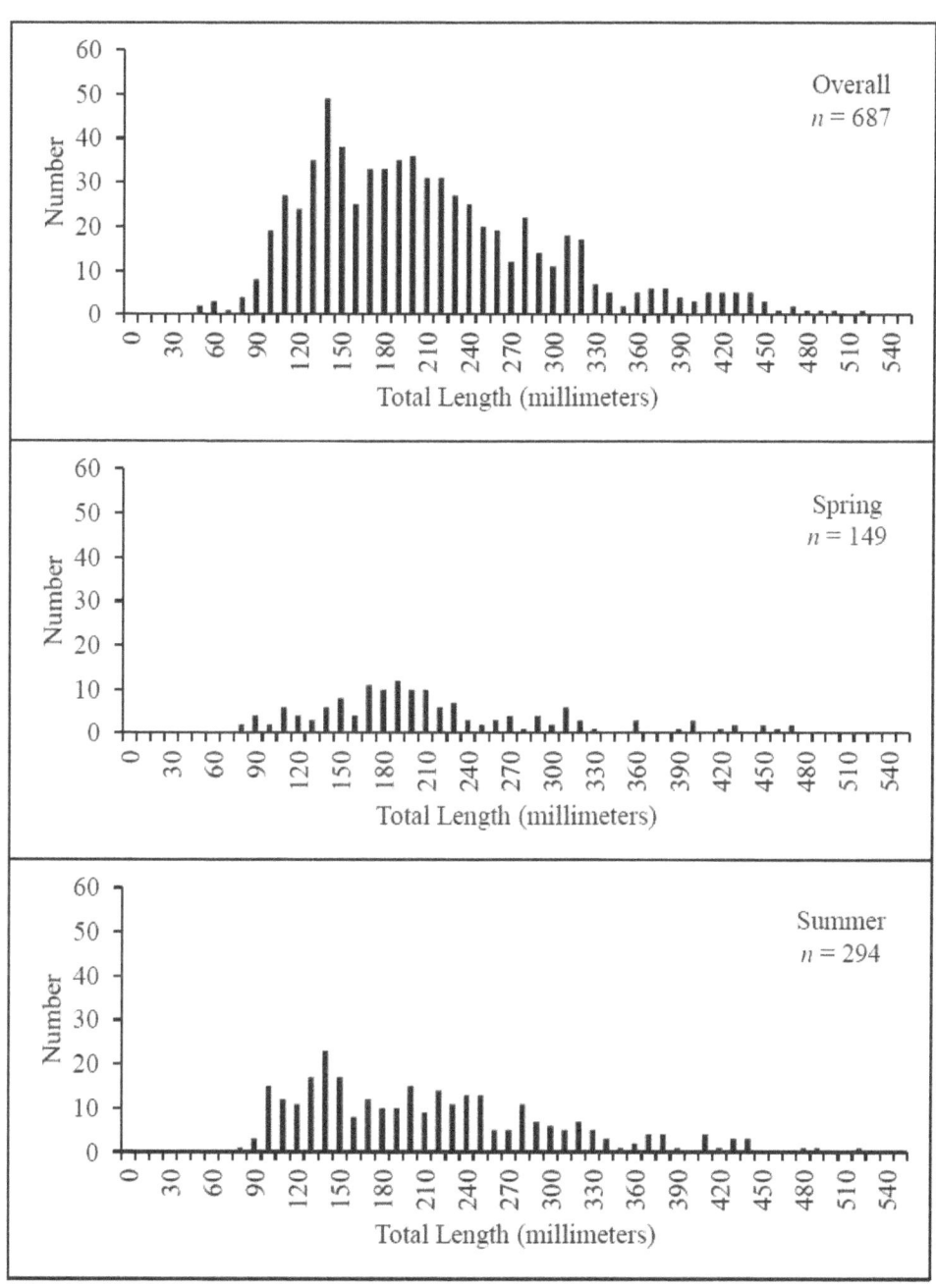

Figure 14. Length frequency histograms for smallmouth bass during predator index sampling overall in 2010 (May 19–September 3), in spring 2010 (May 19–June 8), and in summer 2010 (June 28–August 11), Priest Rapids Project, Columbia River, Washington. *n*, total number of fish.

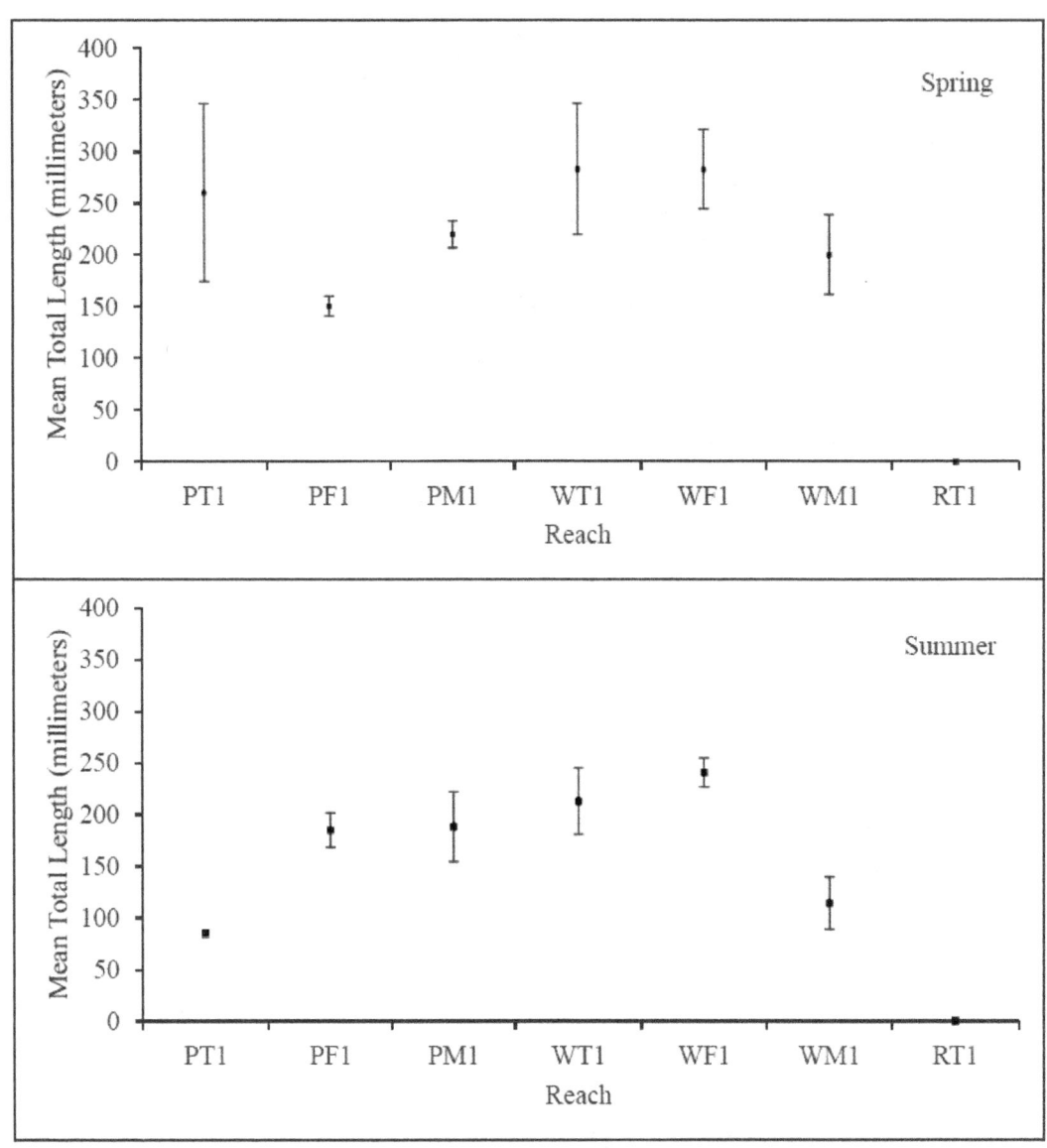

Figure 15. Mean length and one standard error for smallmouth bass during Burley and Poe sampling in spring 2009 (May 27–June 12) and summer 2009 (August 3–20), by reaches, Priest Rapids Project, Columbia River, Washington. Reach locations: PT1, Priest Rapids Tailrace; PF1, Priest Rapids Forebay; PM1, Priest Rapids Mid-Reservoir; WT1, Wanapum Tailrace; WF1, Wanapum Forebay; WM1, Wanapum Mid-Reservoir; RT1, Rock Island Tailrace.

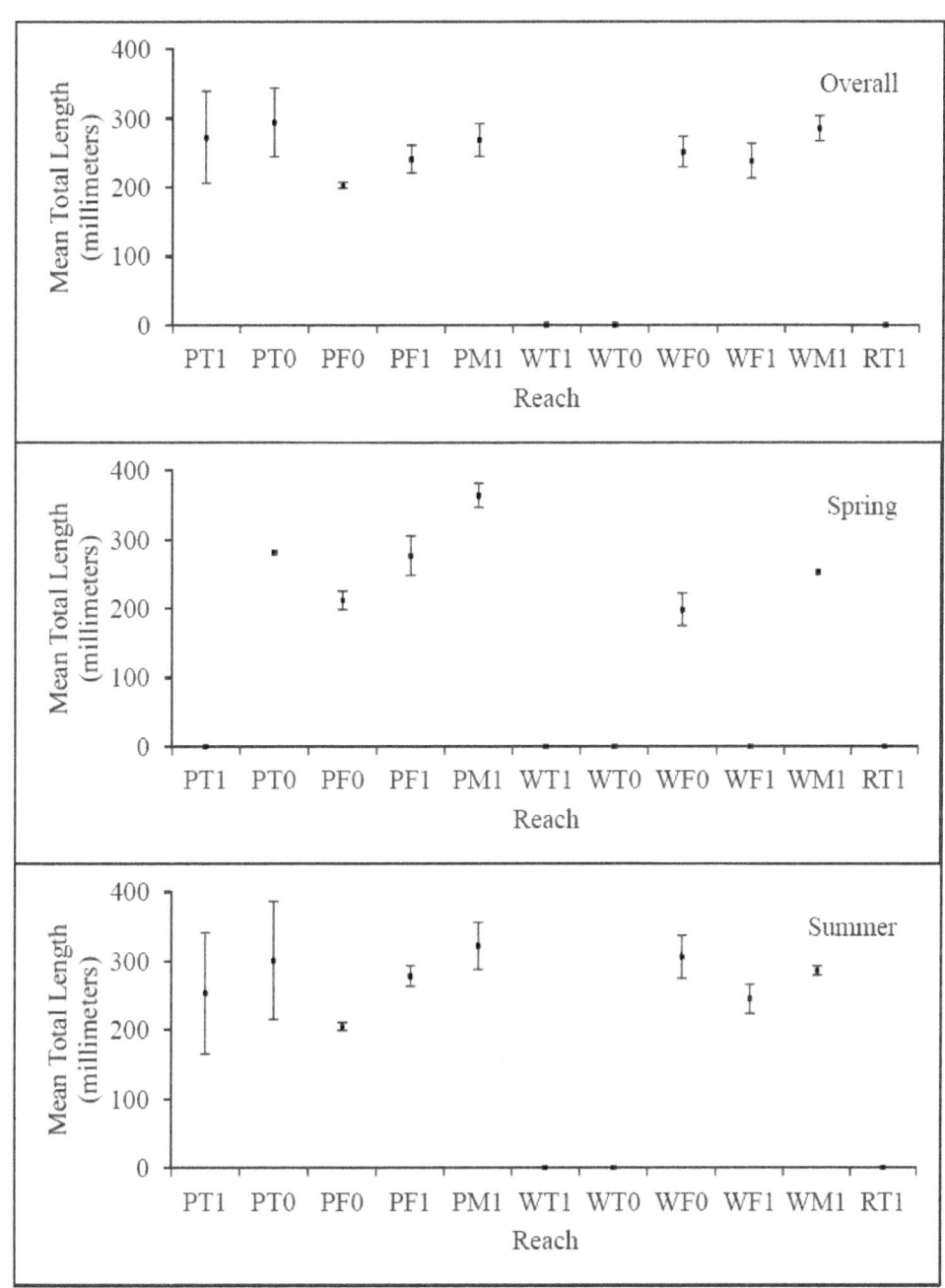

Figure 16. Mean length and one standard error for smallmouth bass during predator index sampling overall in 2009 (May 1–August 27), in spring 2009 (May 7–June 11), and in summer 2009 (June 23–August 5), by reaches, Priest Rapids Project, Columbia River, Washington. Reach locations: PT1, Priest Rapids Tailrace; PT0, Priest Rapids Tailrace BRZ; PF0, Priest Rapids Forebay BRZ; PF1, Priest Rapids Forebay; PM1, Priest Rapids Mid-Reservoir; WT1, Wanapum Tailrace; WT0, Wanapum Tailrace BRZ; WF0, Wanapum Forebay BRZ; WF1, Wanapum Forebay; WM1, Wanapum Mid-Reservoir; RT1, Rock Island Tailrace.

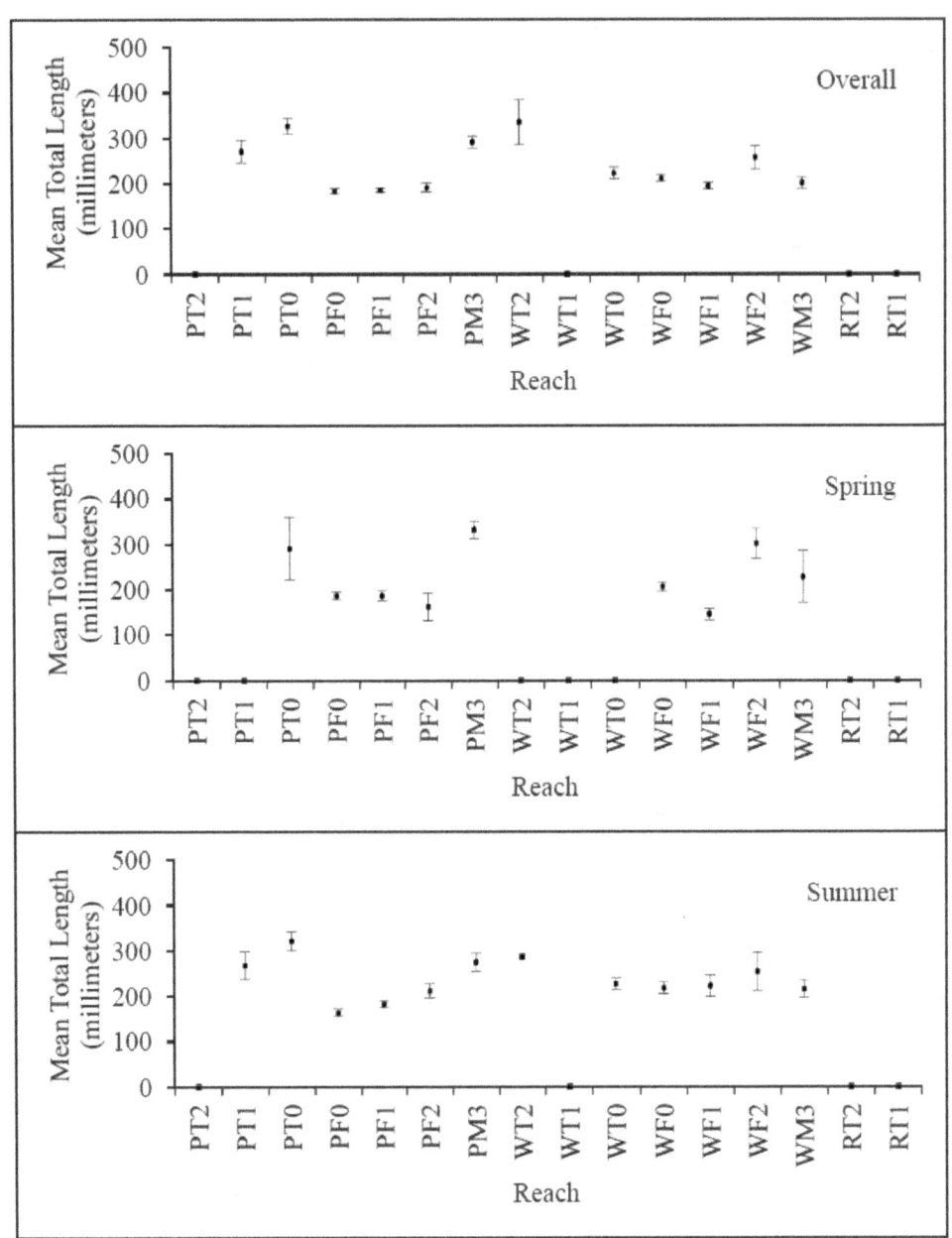

Figure 17. Mean length and one standard error for smallmouth bass during predator index sampling overall in 2010 (May 19–September 3), in spring 2010 (May 19–June 8), and in summer 2010 (June 28–August 11), by reaches, Priest Rapids Project, Columbia River, Washington. Reach locations: PT2, Priest Rapids Tailrace; PT1, Priest Rapids Tailrace near-BRZ; PT0, Priest Rapids Tailrace BRZ; PF0, Priest Rapids Forebay BRZ; PF1, Priest Rapids Forebay near-BRZ; PF2, Priest Rapids Forebay; PM3, Priest Rapids Mid-Reservoir; WT2, Wanapum Tailrace; WT1, Wanapum Tailrace near-BRZ; WT0, Wanapum Tailrace BRZ; WF0, Wanapum Forebay BRZ; WF1, Wanapum Forebay near-BRZ; WF2, Wanapum Forebay; WM3, Wanapum Mid-Reservoir; RT2, Rock Island Tailrace; RT1, Rock Island Tailrace near-BRZ.

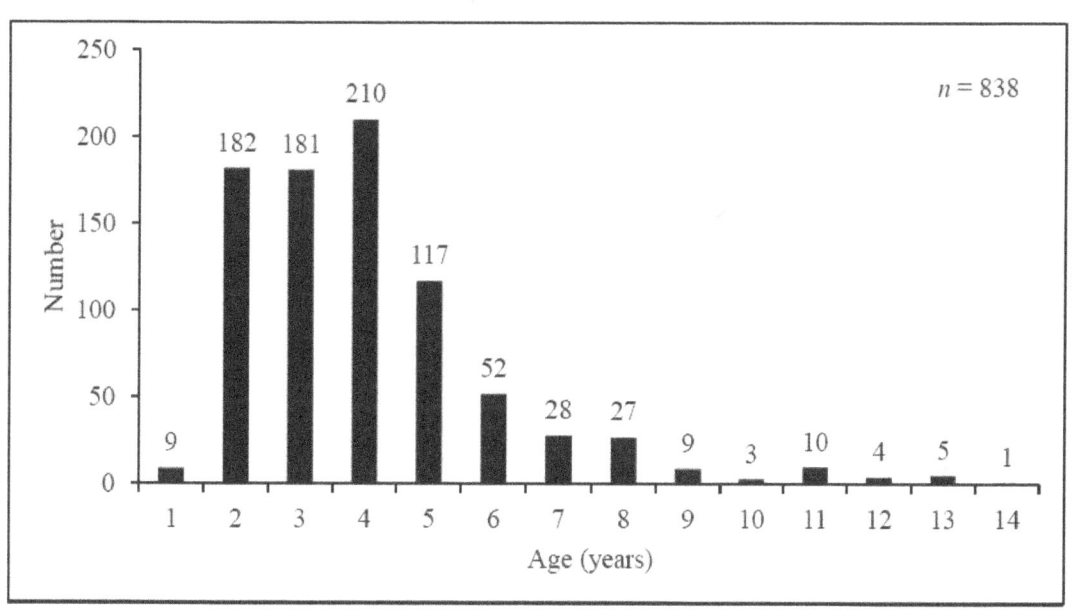

Figure 18. Age frequency (number) of smallmouth bass captured, Priest Rapids Project, Columbia River, Washington, 2009–11. *n*, total number of fish.

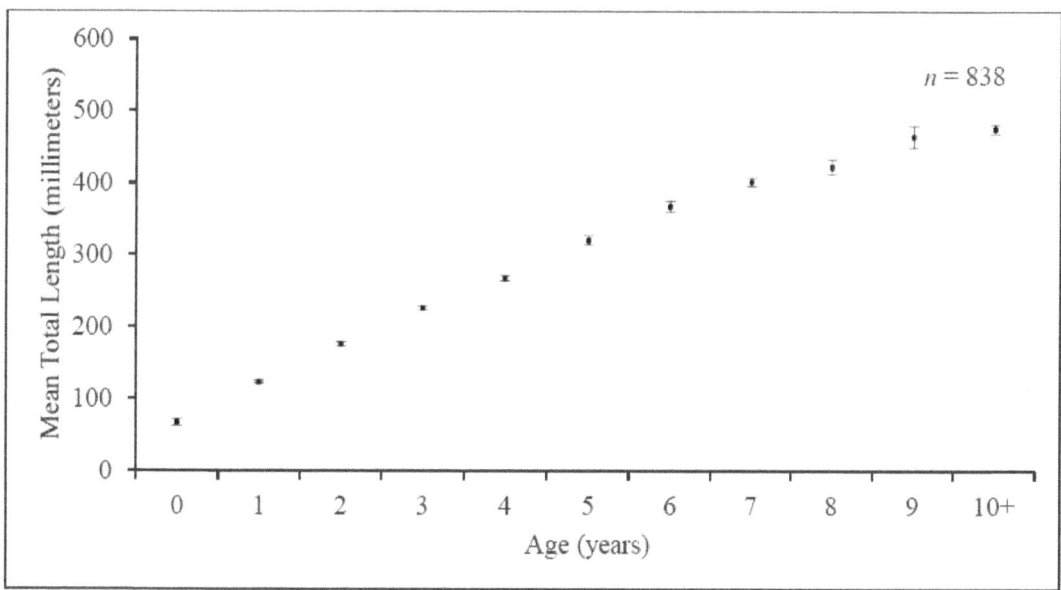

Figure 19. Mean length at age and one standard error for smallmouth bass captured Priest Rapids Project, Columbia River, Washington, 2009–11. Fish 10 years old and older are combined. *n*, total number of fish.

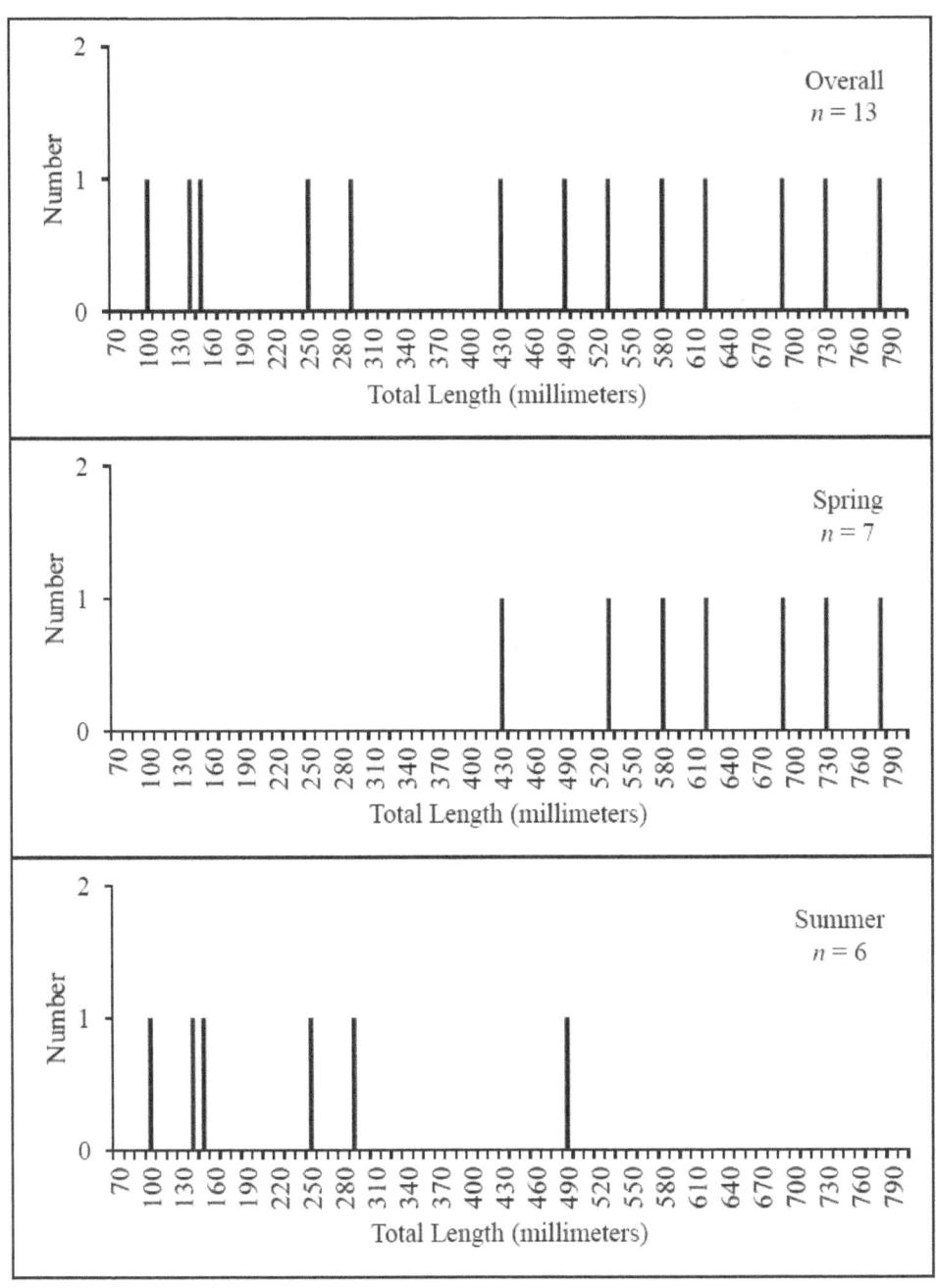

Figure 20. Length frequency histograms for walleye during Burley and Poe sampling overall in 2009 (May 27–June 12 and August 3–20), in spring 2009 (May 27–June 12), and in summer 2009 (August 3–20), Priest Rapids Project, Columbia River, Washington. *n*, total number of fish.

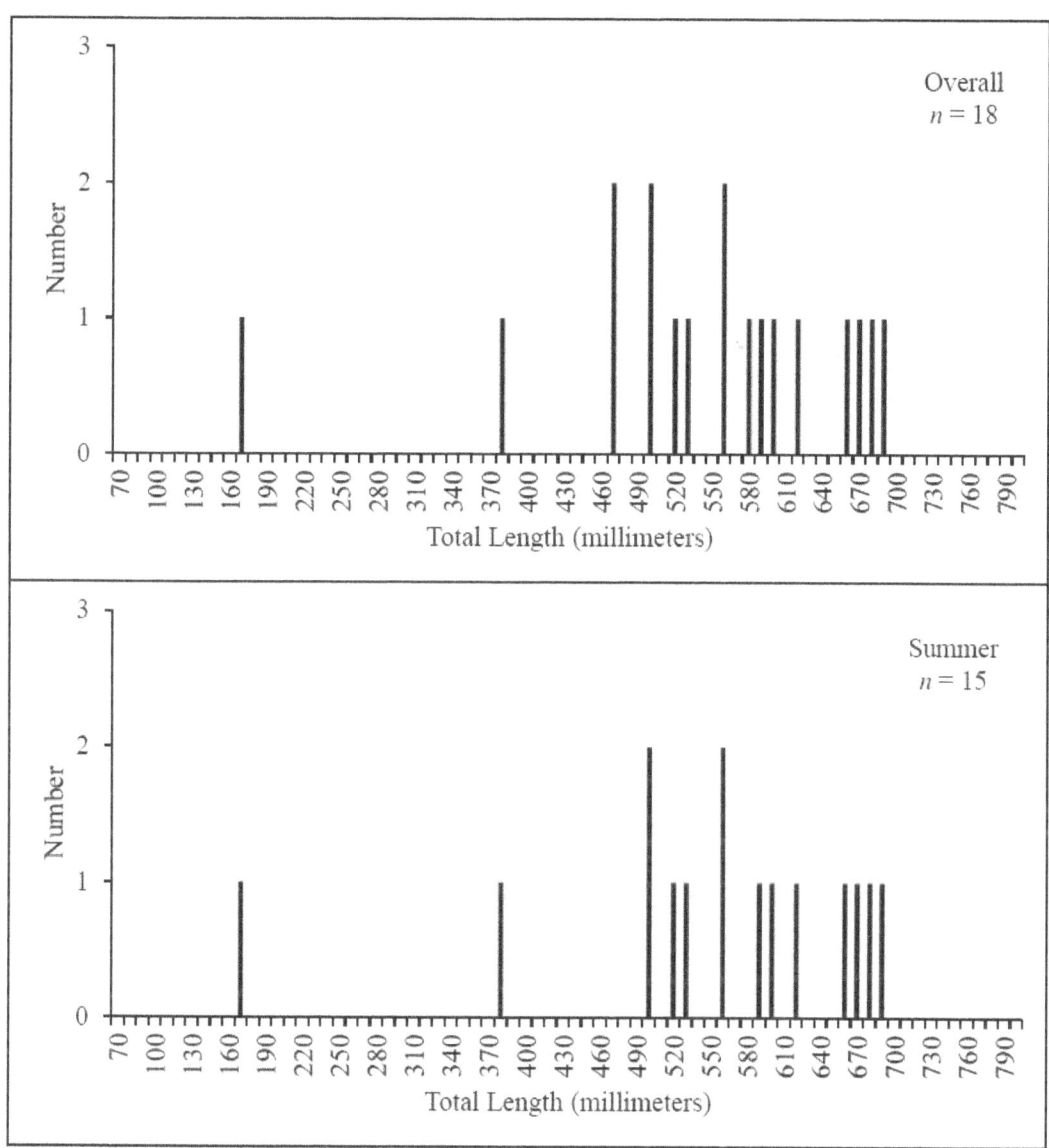

Figure 21. Length frequency histogram for walleye during predator index sampling overall in 2009 (May 1–August 27), and in summer 2009 (August 3–20), Priest Rapids Project, Columbia River, Washington. There were not enough fish captured in 2009 during night electrofishing sampling to generate length frequency histograms for spring or by reservoir. *n*, total number of fish.

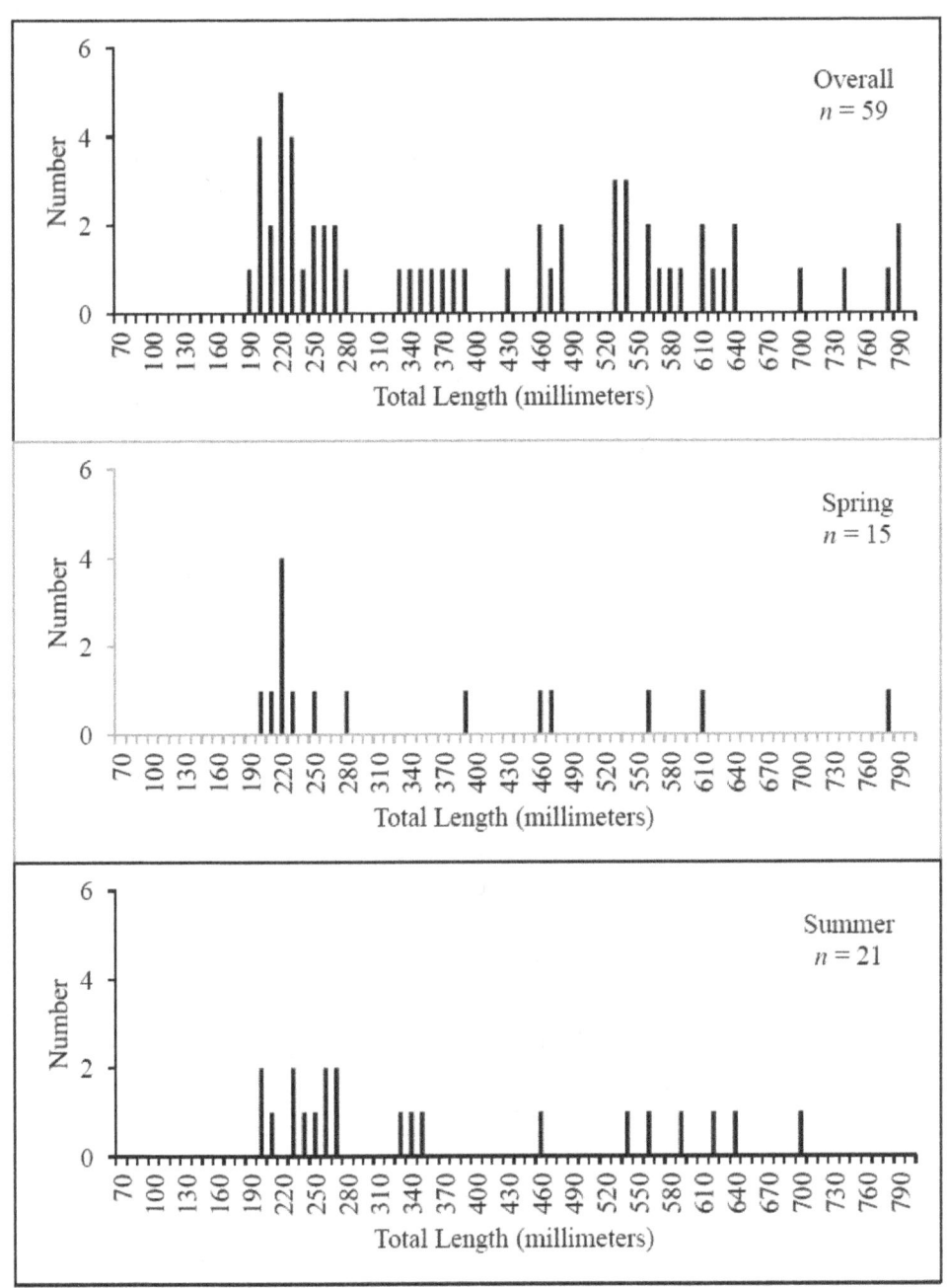

Figure 22. Length frequency histograms for walleye during predator index sampling overall in 2010 (May 19–September 3), in spring 2010 (May 19–June 8), and in summer 2010 (June 28–August 11), Priest Rapids Project, Columbia River, Washington. *n*, total number of fish.

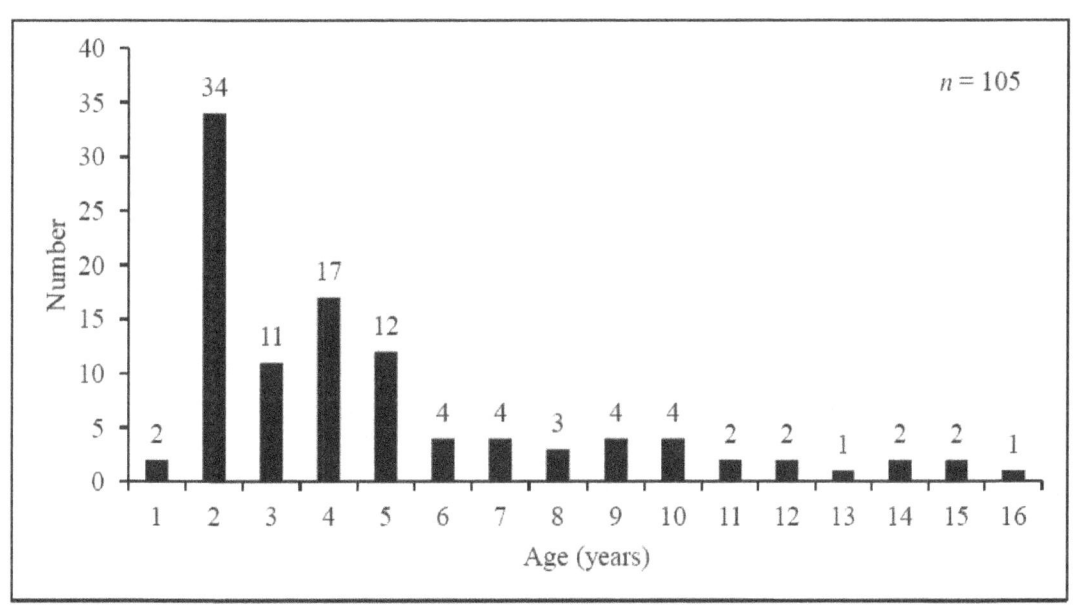

Figure 23. Age frequency (number) of walleye captured, Priest Rapids Project, Columbia River, Washington, 2009–11. *n*, total number of fish.

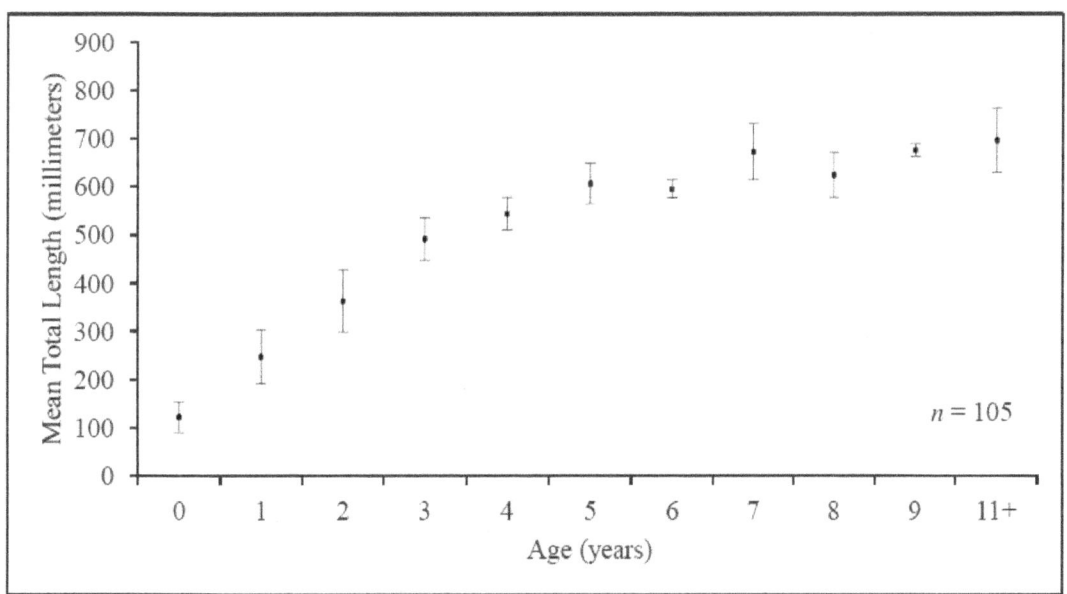

Figure 24. Mean length at age and one standard error for walleye captured, Priest Rapids Project, Columbia River, Washington, 2009–11. Fish 11 years old and older are combined. *n*, total number of fish.

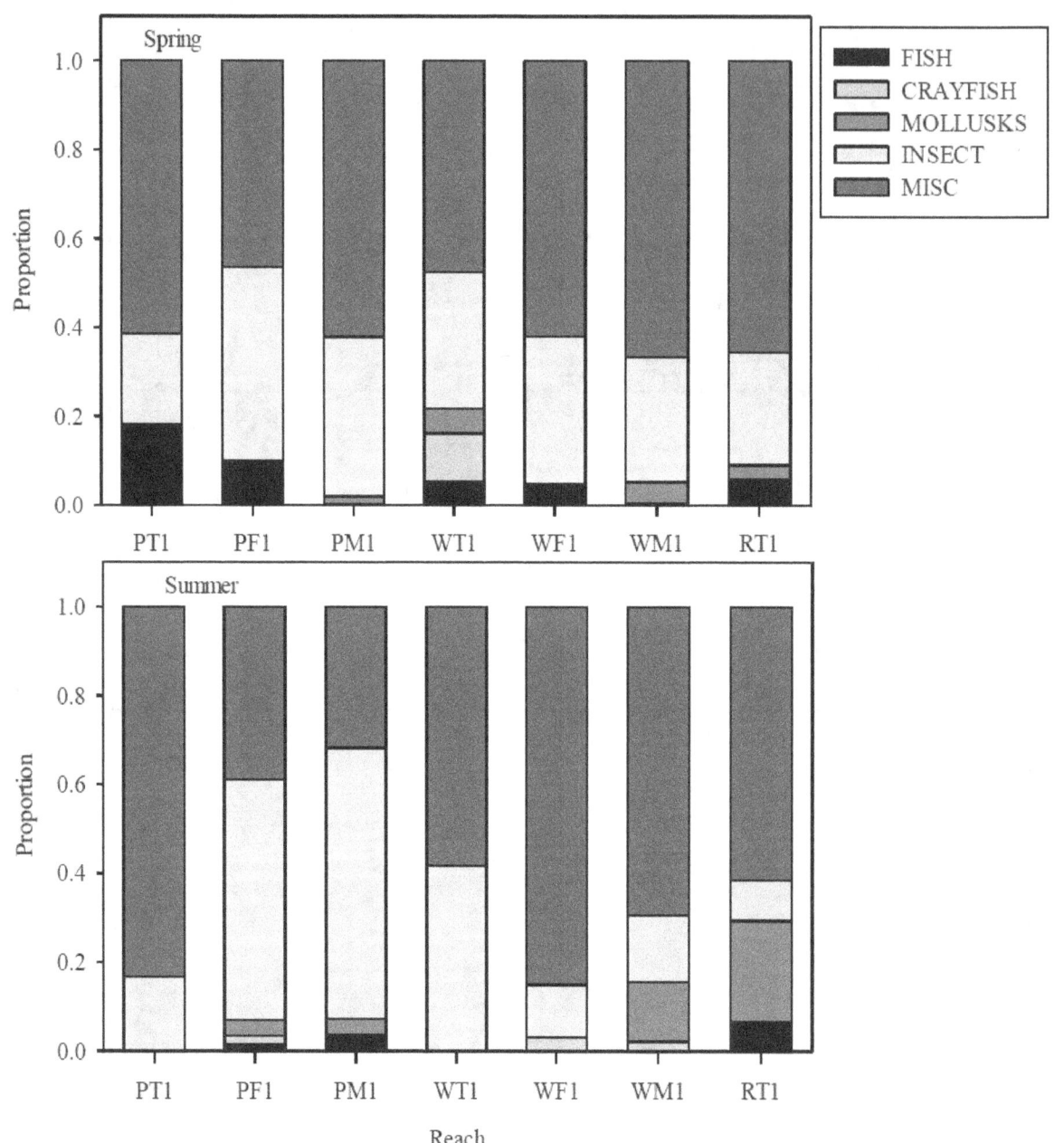

Figure 25. Proportion of diet for northern pikeminnow during Burley and Poe sampling in spring 2009 (May 27–June 12) and summer 2009 (August 3–20), by reaches, Priest Rapids Project, Columbia River, Washington. Reaches with no column indicate no diet sample. Reach locations: PT1, Priest Rapids Tailrace; PF1, Priest Rapids Forebay; PM1, Priest Rapids Mid-Reservoir; WT1, Wanapum Tailrace; WF1, Wanapum Forebay; WM1, Wanapum Mid-Reservoir; RT1, Rock Island Tailrace.

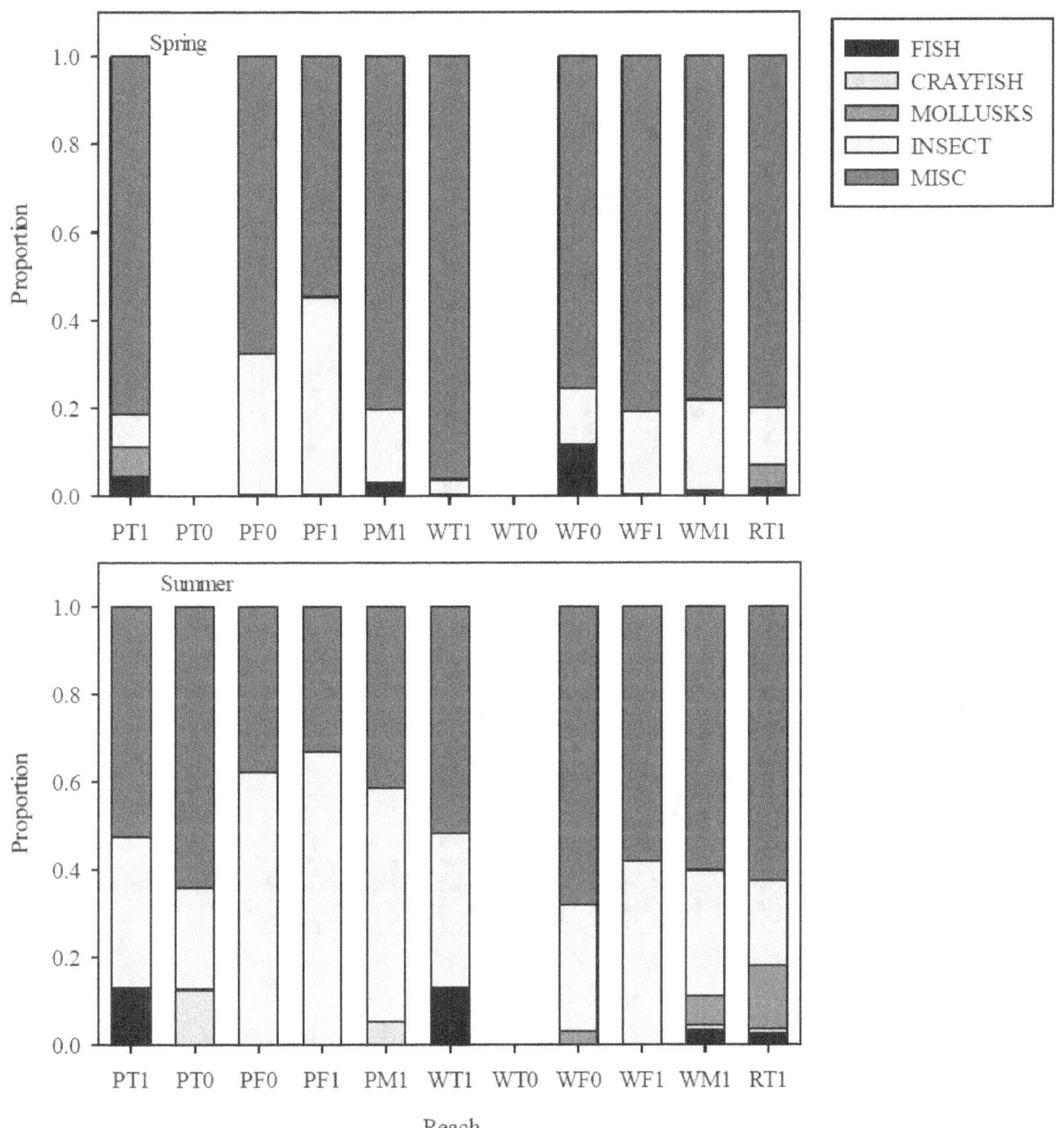

Figure 26. Proportion of diet for northern pikeminnow during Predator index sampling in spring 2009 (May 7–June 11) and summer 2009 (June 23 - August 5), by reaches, Priest Rapids Project, Columbia River, Washington. Reaches with no column indicate no diet sample. Reach locations: PT1, Priest Rapids Tailrace; PT0, Priest Rapids Tailrace BRZ; PF0, Priest Rapids Forebay BRZ; PF1, Priest Rapids Forebay; PM1, Priest Rapids Mid-Reservoir; WT1, Wanapum Tailrace; WT0, Wanapum Tailrace BRZ; WF0, Wanapum Forebay BRZ; WF1, Wanapum Forebay; WM1, Wanapum Mid-Reservoir; RT1, Rock Island Tailrace.

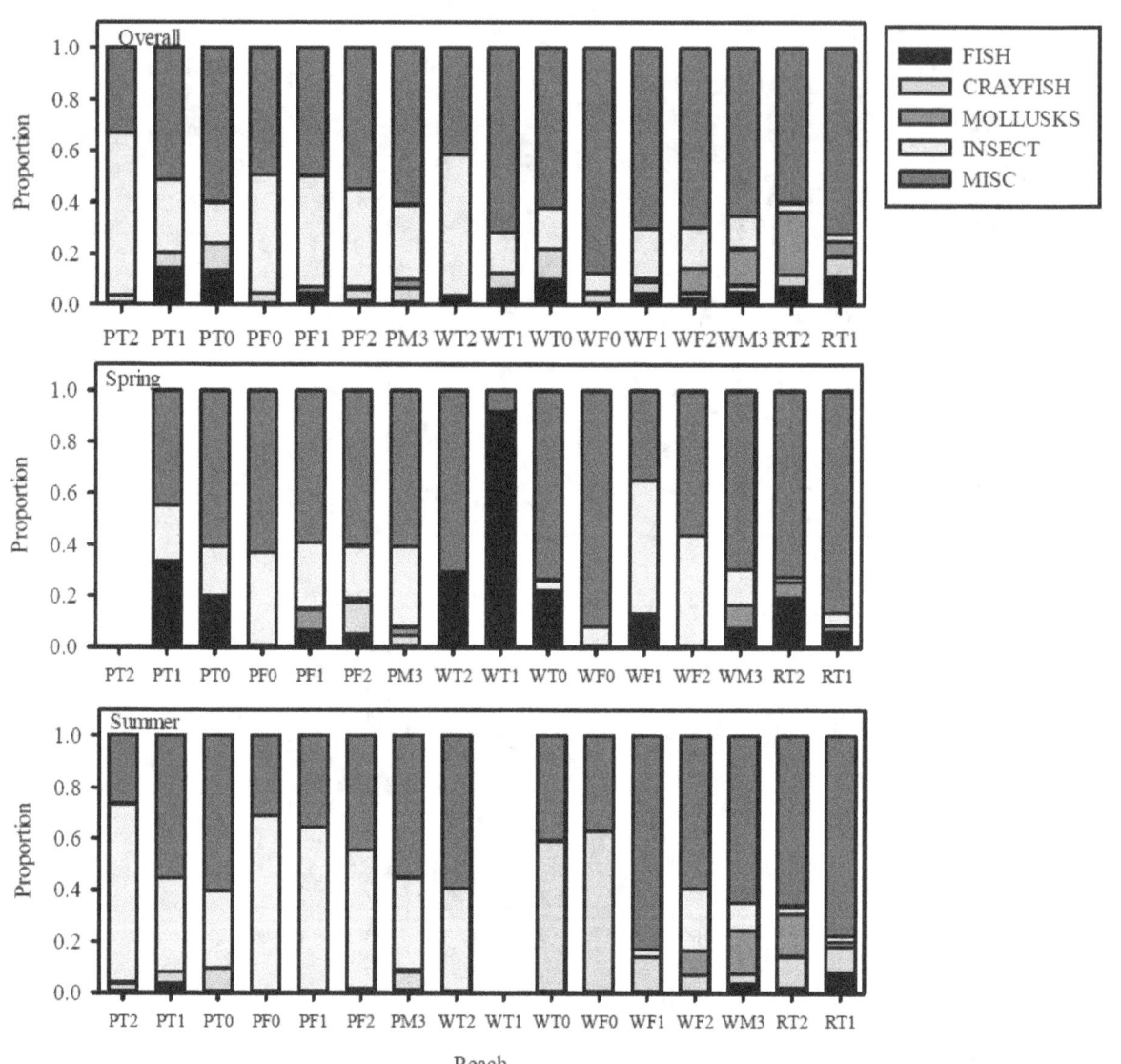

Figure 27. Proportion of diet of northern pikeminnow collected during predator index sampling overall in 2010 (May 19–September 3), in spring 2010 (May 2–June 9), and in summer 2010 (June 27–August 11), by reaches, Priest Rapids Project, Columbia River, Washington. Reaches with no column indicate no diet sample. Reach locations: PT2, Priest Rapids Tailrace; PT1, Priest Rapids Tailrace near-BRZ; PT0, Priest Rapids Tailrace BRZ; PF0, Priest Rapids Forebay BRZ; PF1, Priest Rapids Forebay near-BRZ; PF2, Priest Rapids Forebay; PM3, Priest Rapids Mid-Reservoir; WT2, Wanapum Tailrace; WT1, Wanapum Tailrace near-BRZ; WT0, Wanapum Tailrace BRZ; WF0, Wanapum Forebay BRZ; WF1, Wanapum Forebay near-BRZ; WF2, Wanapum Forebay; WM3, Wanapum Mid-Reservoir; RT2, Rock Island Tailrace; RT1, Rock Island Tailrace near-BRZ.

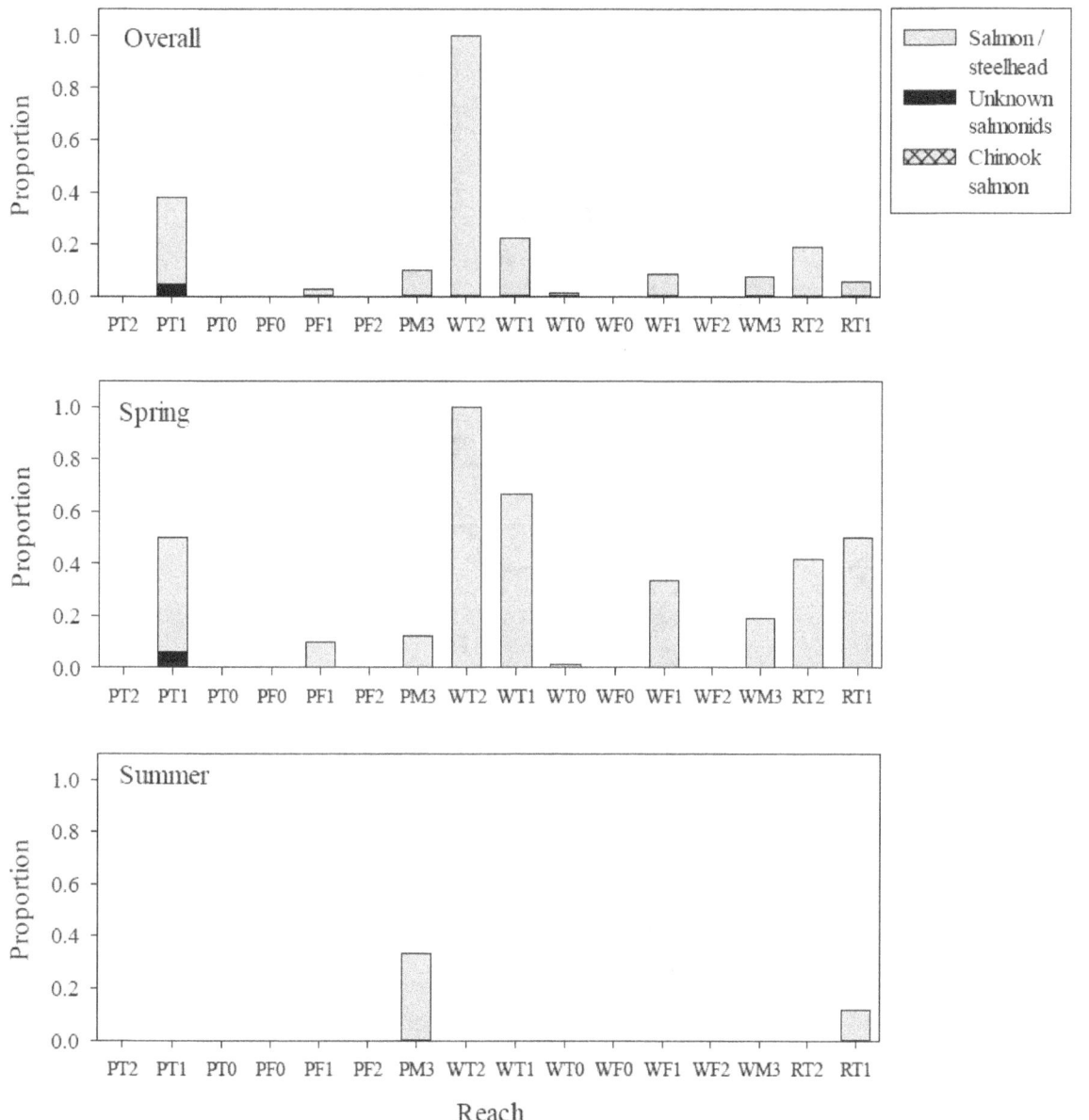

Figure 28. Proportion of fish that are salmon in the diets of northern pikeminnow during predator index sampling in 2010 overall (May 19–September 3), in spring 2010 (May 2–June 9), and summer 2010 (June 27 - August 11), by reach, Priest Rapids Project, Columbia River, Washington. Reach locations: PT2, Priest Rapids Tailrace; PT1, Priest Rapids Tailrace near-BRZ; PT0, Priest Rapids Tailrace BRZ; PF0, Priest Rapids Forebay BRZ; PF1, Priest Rapids Forebay near-BRZ; PF2, Priest Rapids Forebay; PM3, Priest Rapids Mid-Reservoir; WT2, Wanapum Tailrace; WT1, Wanapum Tailrace near-BRZ; WT0, Wanapum Tailrace BRZ; WF0, Wanapum Forebay BRZ; WF1, Wanapum Forebay near-BRZ; WF2, Wanapum Forebay; WM3, Wanapum Mid-Reservoir; RT2, Rock Island Tailrace; RT1, Rock Island Tailrace near-BRZ.

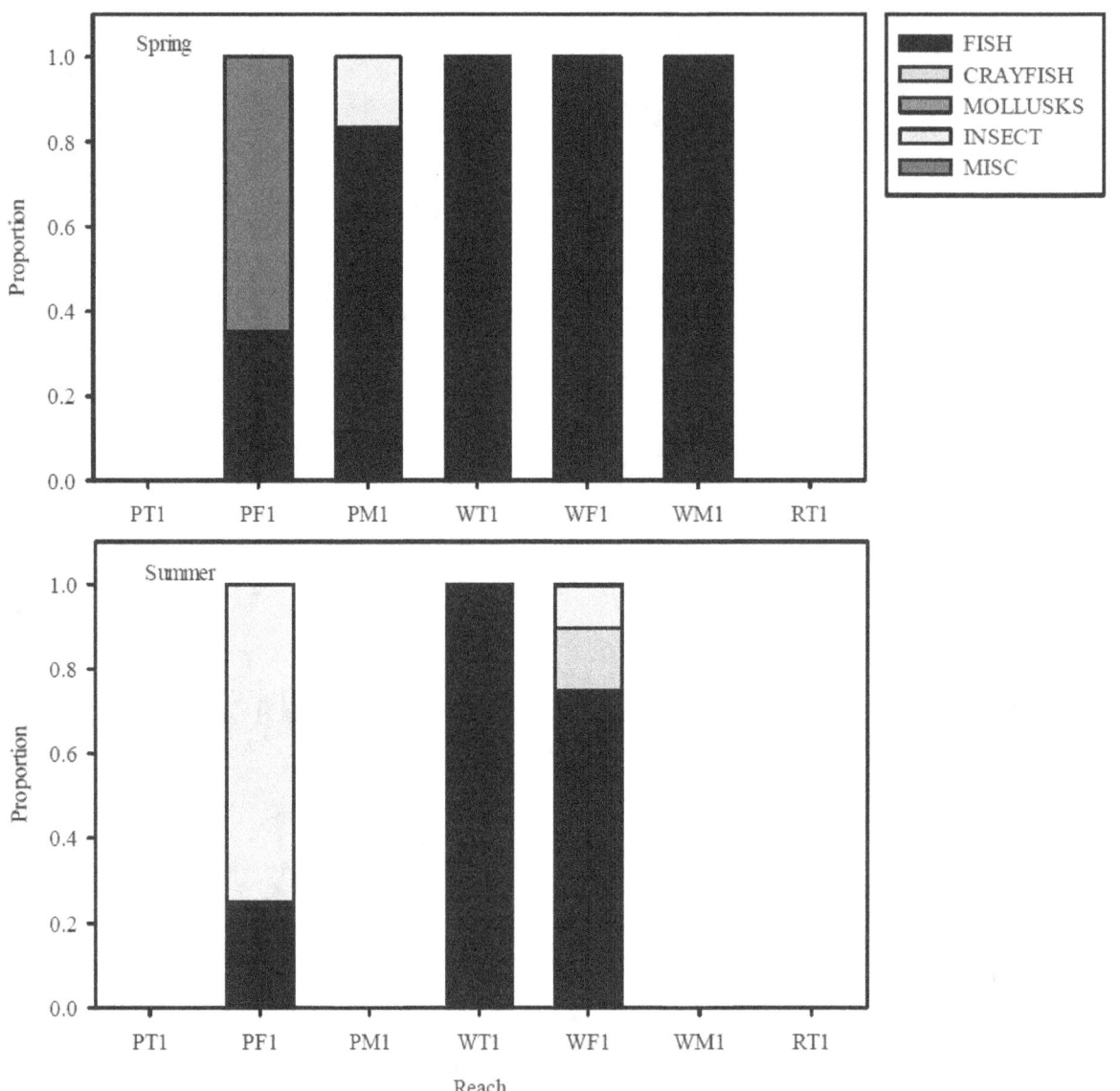

Figure 29. Proportion of diet for smallmouth bass during Burley and Poe sampling in spring 2009 (May 27–June 12) and in summer 2009 (August 3–20), by reaches, Priest Rapids Project, Columbia River, Washington. Reaches with no column indicate no diet sample. Reach locations: PT1, Priest Rapids Tailrace; PF1, Priest Rapids Forebay; PM1, Priest Rapids Mid-Reservoir; WT1, Wanapum Tailrace; WF1, Wanapum Forebay; WM1, Wanapum Mid-Reservoir; RT1, Rock Island Tailrace.

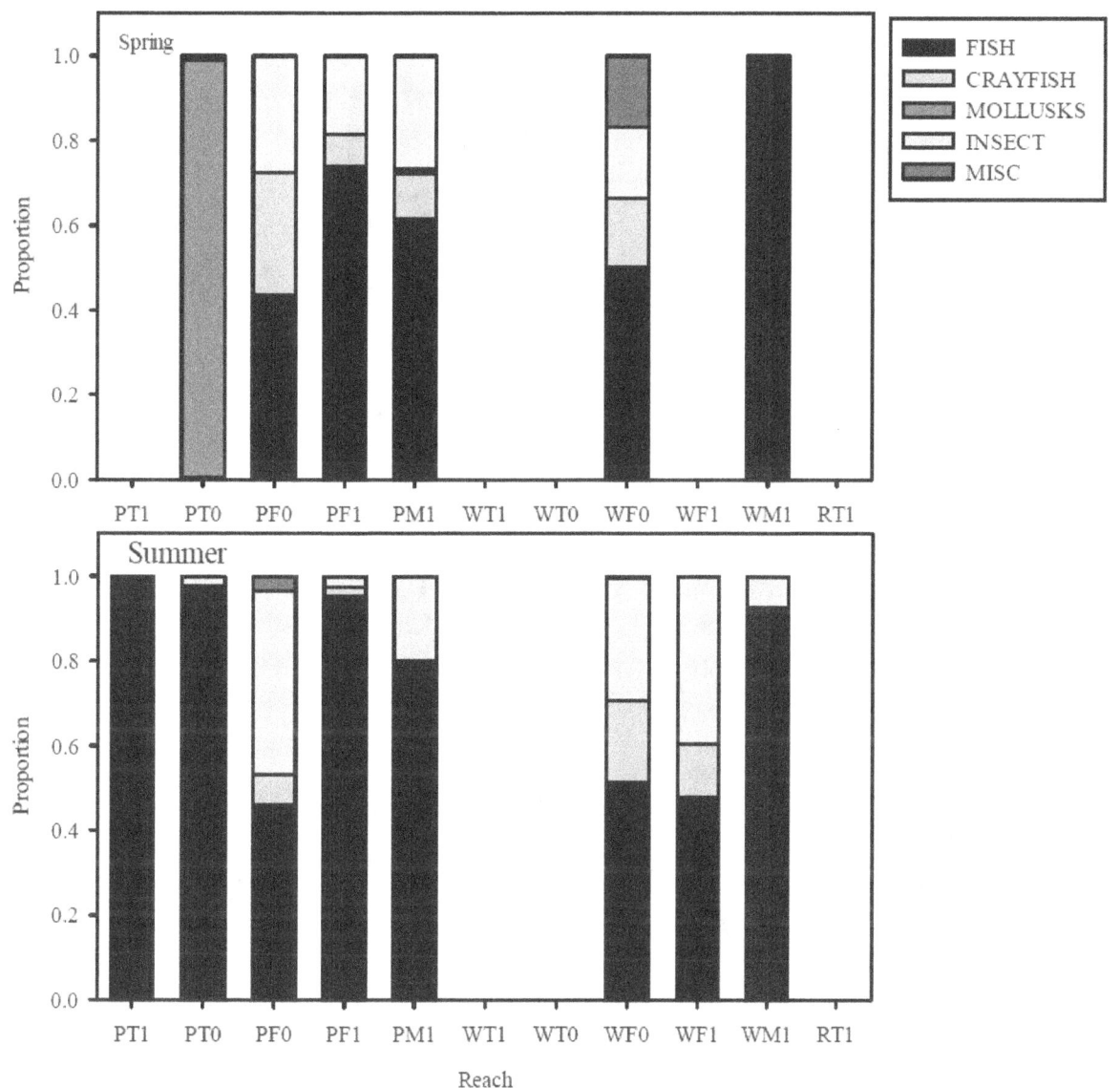

Figure 30. Proportion of diet for smallmouth bass during predator index sampling in spring 2009 (May 7–June 11) and summer 2009 (June 23 - August 5), by reaches, Priest Rapids Project, Columbia River, Washington. Reaches with no column indicate no diet sample. Reach locations: PT1, Priest Rapids Tailrace; PT0, Priest Rapids Tailrace BRZ; PF0, Priest Rapids Forebay BRZ; PF1, Priest Rapids Forebay; PM1, Priest Rapids Mid-Reservoir; WT1, Wanapum Tailrace; WT0, Wanapum Tailrace BRZ; WF0, Wanapum Forebay BRZ; WF1, Wanapum Forebay; WM1, Wanapum Mid-Reservoir; RT1, Rock Island Tailrace.

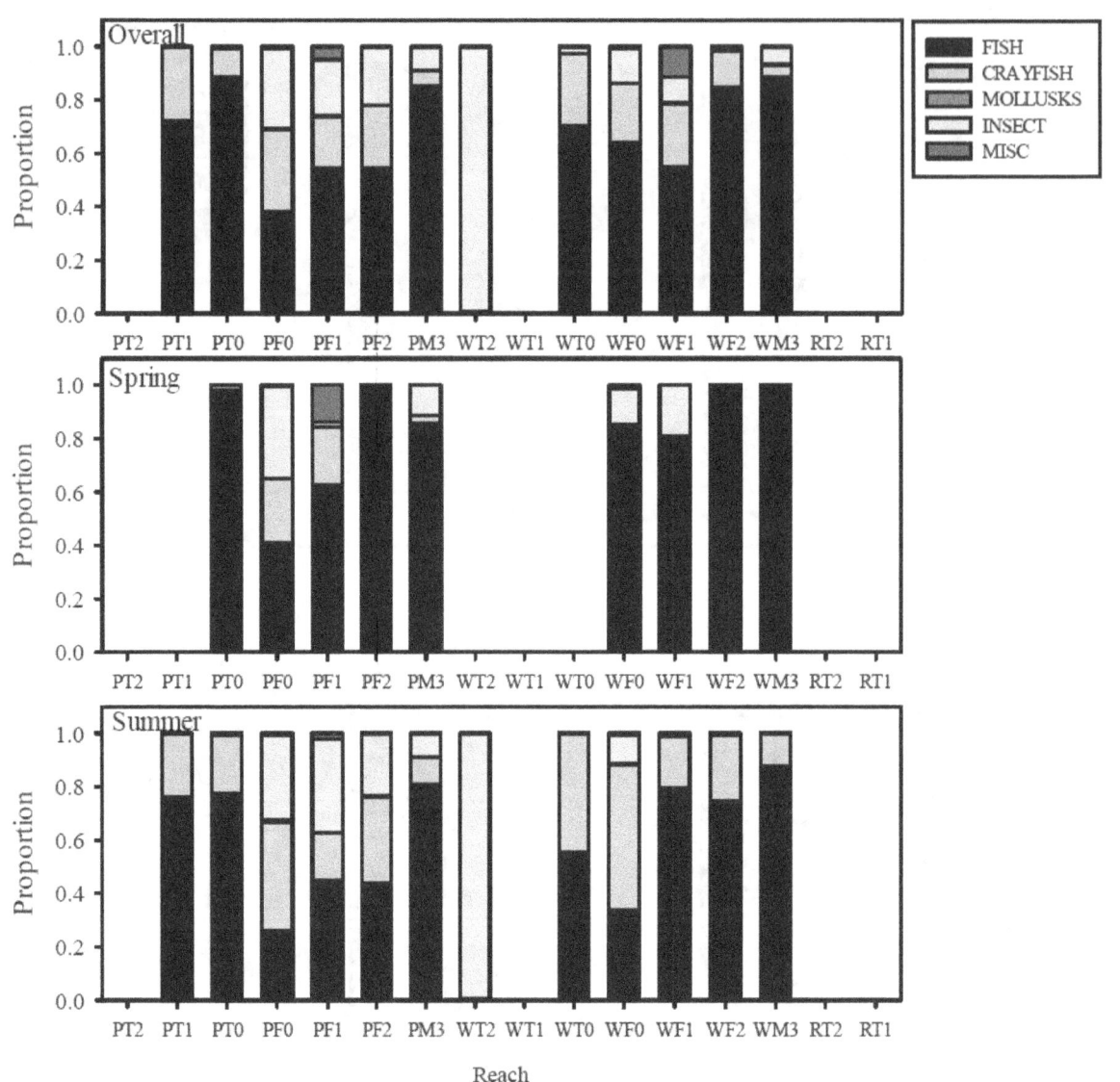

Figure 31. Diet composition of smallmouth bass captured during predator index sampling overall in 2010 (May 19–September 3), in spring 2010 (May 2–June 9), and in summer 2010 (June 27–August 11), by reaches, Priest Rapids Project, Columbia River, Washington. Reaches with no column indicate no diet sample. Reach locations: PT2, Priest Rapids Tailrace; PT1, Priest Rapids Tailrace near-BRZ; PT0, Priest Rapids Tailrace BRZ; PF0, Priest Rapids Forebay BRZ; PF1, Priest Rapids Forebay near-BRZ; PF2, Priest Rapids Forebay; PM3, Priest Rapids Mid-Reservoir; WT2, Wanapum Tailrace; WT1, Wanapum Tailrace near-BRZ; WT0, Wanapum Tailrace BRZ; WF0, Wanapum Forebay BRZ; WF1, Wanapum Forebay near-BRZ; WF2, Wanapum Forebay; WM3, Wanapum Mid-Reservoir; RT2, Rock Island Tailrace; RT1, Rock Island Tailrace near-BRZ.

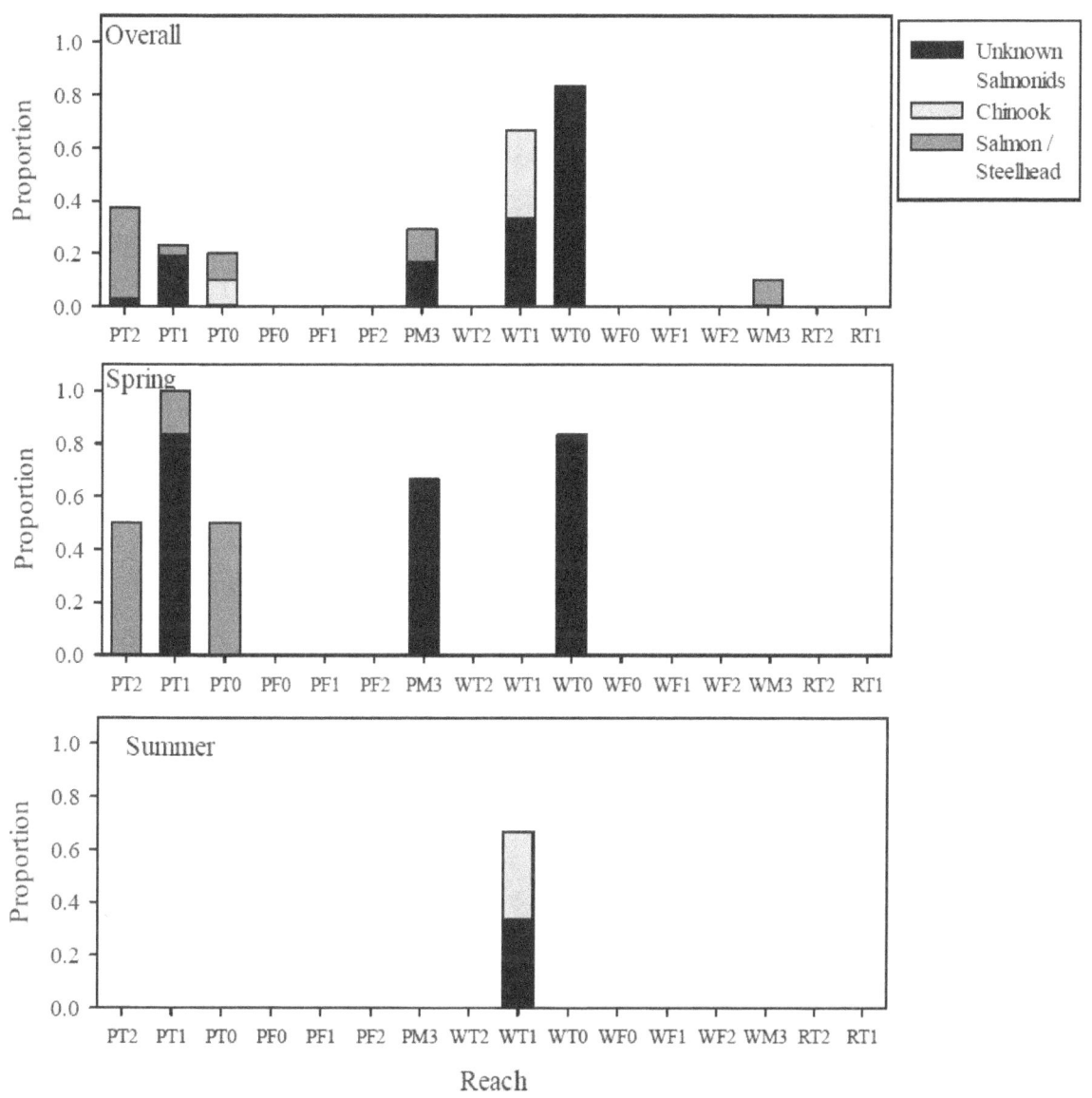

Figure 32. Proportion of fish in diet of walleye that are salmon during predator index sampling overall in 2010 (May 19–September 3), in spring 2010 (May 19– June 8), and in summer 2010 (June 28–August 11) by reaches, Priest Rapids Project, Columbia River, Washington. Reach locations: PT2, Priest Rapids Tailrace; PT1, Priest Rapids Tailrace near-BRZ; PT0, Priest Rapids Tailrace BRZ; PF0, Priest Rapids Forebay BRZ; PF1, Priest Rapids Forebay near-BRZ; PF2, Priest Rapids Forebay; PM3, Priest Rapids Mid-Reservoir; WT2, Wanapum Tailrace; WT1, Wanapum Tailrace near-BRZ; WT0, Wanapum Tailrace BRZ; WF0, Wanapum Forebay BRZ; WF1, Wanapum Forebay near-BRZ; WF2, Wanapum Forebay; WM3, Wanapum Mid-Reservoir; RT2, Rock Island Tailrace; RT1, Rock Island Tailrace near-BRZ.

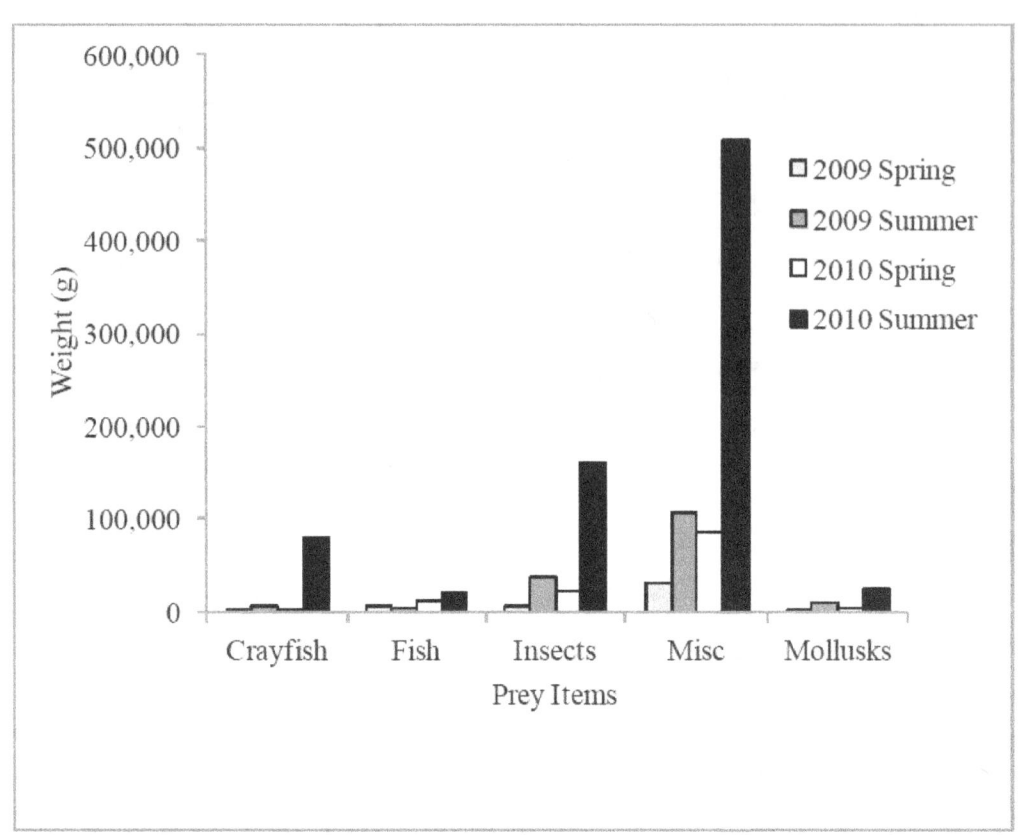

Figure 33. Estimated weights of prey items consumed by northern pikeminnow during the 2009 and 2010 study periods using bioenergetics modeling. Bioenergetics modeling was based on the diets of 928 and 1,118 individuals during the 2009 and 2010 study periods, respectively.

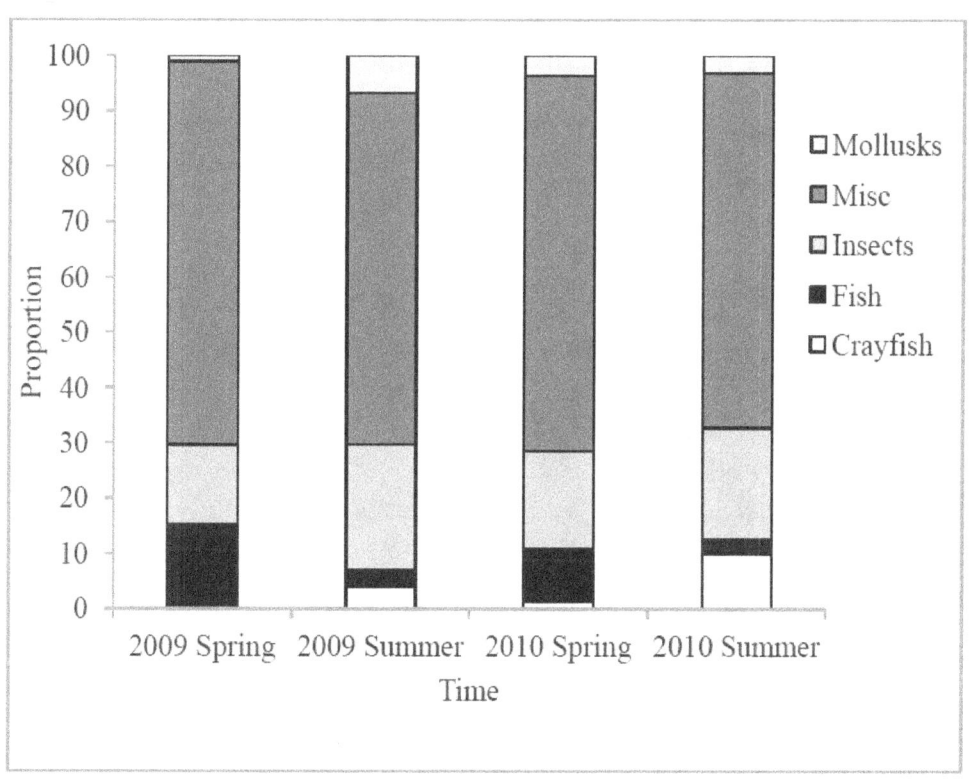

Figure 34. Proportion of prey items consumed by northern pikeminnow from bioenergetics modeling during the 2009 and 2010 study periods. Bioenergetics modeling was based on the diets of 928 and 1,118 individuals during the 2009 and 2010 study periods, respectively.

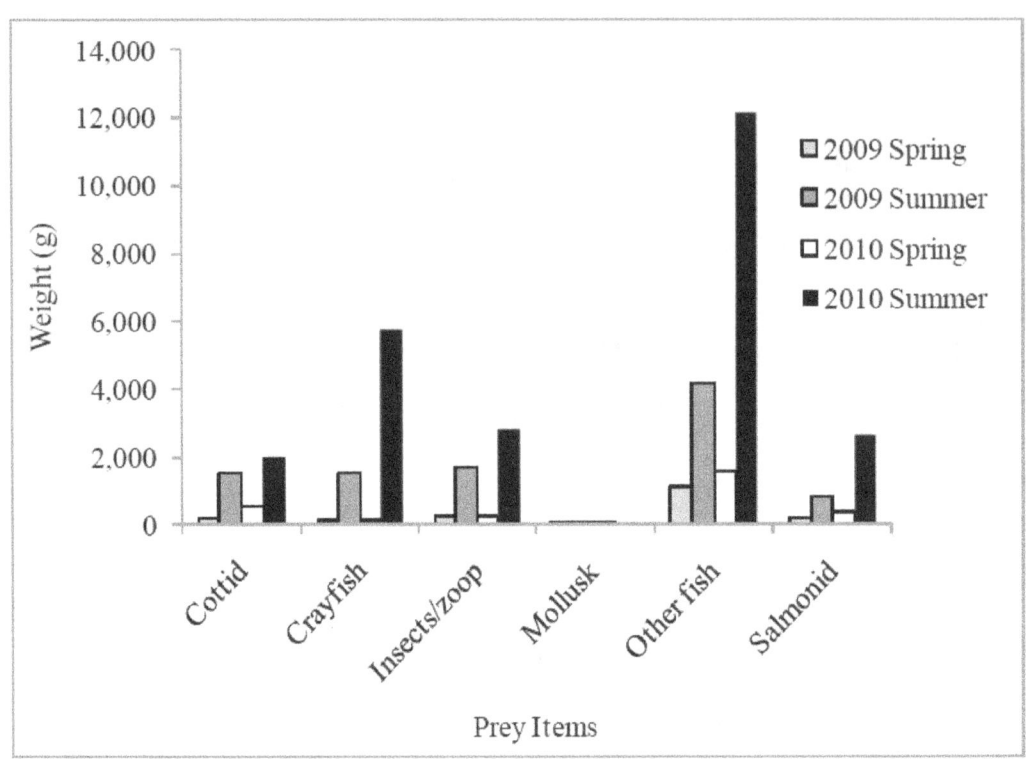

Figure 35. Estimated weights of prey items consumed by smallmouth bass during the 2009 and 2010 study periods using bioenergetics modeling. Bioenergetics modeling was based on the diets of 165 and 372 individuals during the 2009 and 2010 study periods, respectively.

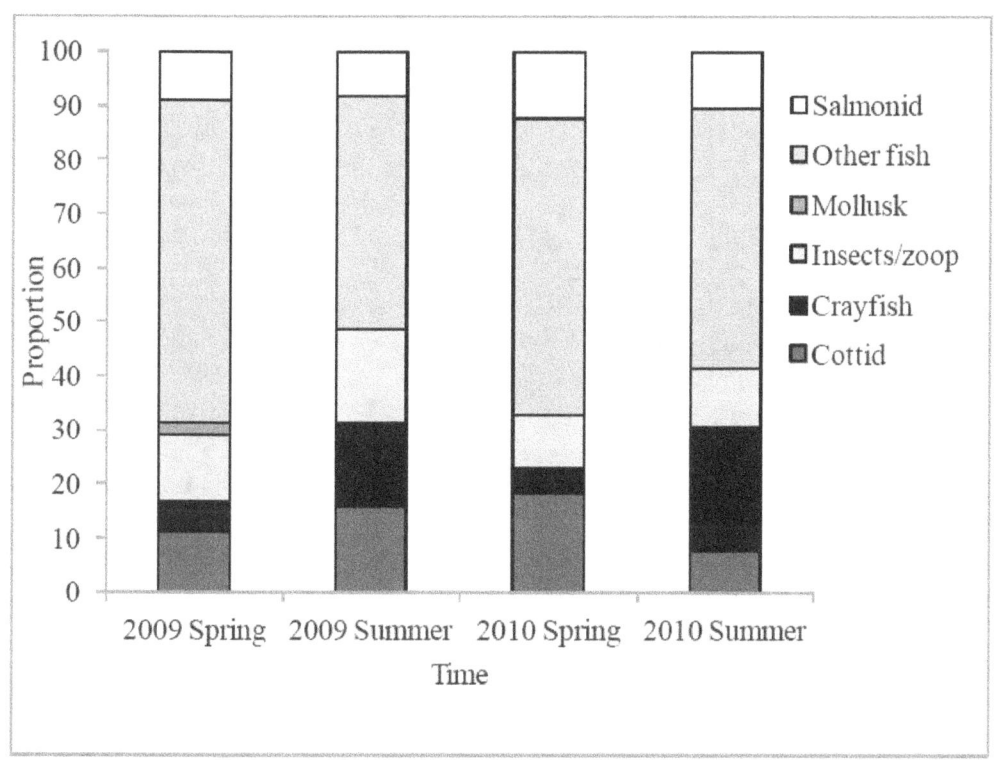

Figure 36. Proportion of prey items consumed by smallmouth bass from bioenergetics modeling during the 2009 and 2010 study periods. Bioenergetics modeling was based on the diets of 165 and 372 individuals during the 2009 and 2010 study periods, respectively.

Table 1. Estimated area of each reach that is less than 3 meters in depth, Priest Rapids Project, Columbia River, Washington, 2009–10.

[BRZ, Boat Restricted Zone in the forebay and tailrace of each dam; HA, hectares; <, less than; M, meters]

YEAR	RESERVOIR	REACHES	AREA (HA) < 3 M DEPTH
2009	Hanford	Priest Rapids Tailrace	120.75
2009	Hanford	Priest Rapids Tailrace BRZ	11.11
2009	Priest Rapids	Priest Rapids Forebay BRZ	0.576
2009	Priest Rapids	Priest Rapids Forebay	101.86
2009	Priest Rapids	Priest Rapids Mid-Reservoir	89.18
2009	Priest Rapids	Wanapum Tailrace	174.51
2009	Priest Rapids	Wanapum Tailrace BRZ	2.33
2009	Wanapum	Wanapum Forebay BRZ	4.44
2009	Wanapum	Wanapum Forebay	134.90
2009	Wanapum	Wanapum Mid-Reservoir	74.88
2009	Wanapum	Rock Island Tailrace	30.46
2010	Hanford	Priest Rapids Tailrace	116.73
2010	Hanford	Priest Rapids Tailrace near-BRZ	2.12
2010	Hanford	Priest Rapids Tailrace BRZ	2.82
2010	Priest Rapids	Priest Rapids Forebay BRZ	1.37
2010	Priest Rapids	Priest Rapids Forebay near-BRZ	5.30
2010	Priest Rapids	Priest Rapids Forebay	88.89
2010	Priest Rapids	Priest Rapids Mid-Reservoir	176.21
2010	Priest Rapids	Wanapum Tailrace	155.1
2010	Priest Rapids	Wanapum Tailrace near-BRZ	19.71
2010	Priest Rapids	Wanapum Tailrace BRZ	3.16
2010	Wanapum	Wanapum Forebay BRZ	3.36
2010	Wanapum	Wanapum Forebay near-BRZ	4.11
2010	Wanapum	Wanapum Forebay	133.37
2010	Wanapum	Wanapum Mid-Reservoir	295.37
2010	Wanapum	Rock Island Tailrace	28.13
2010	Wanapum	Rock Island Tailrace near-BRZ	2.39

Table 2. Percentage of each age class of northern pikeminnow and smallmouth bass captured in 2009 and 2010 in less than 3 m depth in the Priest Rapids Project, Columbia River, Washington.

[Composition is based on the total number of each species sampled during the field season]

Age	2009		2010	
	Northern Pikeminnow	Smallmouth Bass	Northern Pikeminnow	Smallmouth Bass
0	54.0			
1	14.2		12.5	
2	7.5	30.9	13.6	36.6
3	7.0	26.1	24.2	24.2
4	5.4	21.2	19.7	16.9
5	4.2	14.5	12.8	12.1
6	2.6	7.3	7.0	4.8
7	1.6		3.9	1.9
8	1.4		2.7	3.5
9	2.0		3.6	

Table 3. Catch of northern pikeminnow in 10 minute period during Burley and Poe sampling in spring (May 27–June 12) and summer (August 3–20), and during predator index sampling in spring (May 7–June 11) and summer (June 23 - August 5), by reaches, Priest Rapids Project, Columbia River, Washington, 2009.

[Catch per unit effort for Burley and Poe (2009) represents catches of northern pikeminnow greater than 250 millimeters and smallmouth bass greater than 150 millimeters, and for Predator Index 2009 represents catches of northern pikeminnow greater than 170 mm and smallmouth bass greater than 150 millimeters. Reach locations: PT1, Priest Rapids Tailrace; PT0, Priest Rapids Tailrace BRZ (Boat Restricted Zone); PF0, Priest Rapids Forebay BRZ; PF1, Priest Rapids Forebay; PM3, Priest Rapids Mid-Reservoir; WT1, Wanapum Tailrace; WT0, Wanapum Tailrace BRZ; WF0, Wanapum Forebay BRZ; WF1, Wanapum Forebay; WM3, Wanapum Mid-Reservoir; RT1, Rock Island Tailrace]

	Catch per 10 minutes							
	Northern pikeminnow				Smallmouth bass			
	Burley and Poe 2009		Predator Index 2009		Burley and Poe 2009		Predator Index 2009	
Reaches	Spring	Summer	Spring	Summer	Spring	Summer	Spring	Summer
PT1	0.004	0.002	0.012	0.011	0.001	0	0	0.002
PT0	a	a	0^b	0.020	a	a	0.010	0.012
PF0	a	a	0.007	0.010	a	a	0.033	0.098
PF1	0.004	0.018	0.009	0.005	0.015	0.012	0.012	0.012
PM3	0.010	0.023	0.026	0.009	0.019	0.003	0.020	0.007
WT1	0.002	0.002	0.003	0.005	0.002	0.002	0	0
WT0	a	a	0^b	c	a	a	0	c
WF0	a	a	0.075	0.040	a	a	0.030	0.035
WF1	0.021	0.013	0	0.016	0.007	0.017	0	0.008
WM3	0.022	0.028	0.039	0.036	0.003	0.0004	0.001	0.006
RT1	0.026	0.038	0.072	0.037	0	0	0	0

a- Boat restricted zones were not sampled as part of the 2009 Burley and Poe sampling due to logistical restraints.

b- Only one electrofishing effort was conducted.

c- Not sampled.

Table 4. Catch of northern pikeminnow (greater than 170 millimeters in length) and smallmouth bass (greater than 150 millimeters in length) per 10 minute period captured during electrofishing runs in spring (May 2–June 9) and summer 2010 (June 27–August 11), by reaches, Priest Rapids Project, Columbia River, Washington.

[Reach locations: PT2, Priest Rapids Tailrace; PT1, Priest Rapids Tailrace near-BRZ; PT0, Priest Rapids Tailrace BRZ; PF0, Priest Rapids Forebay BRZ; PF1, Priest Rapids Forebay near-BRZ; PF2, Priest Rapids Forebay; PM3, Priest Rapids Mid-Reservoir; WT2, Wanapum Tailrace; WT1, Wanapum Tailrace near-BRZ; WT0, Wanapum Tailrace BRZ; WF0, Wanapum Forebay BRZ; WF1, Wanapum Forebay near-BRZ; WF2, Wanapum Forebay; WM3, Wanapum Mid-Reservoir; RT2, Rock Island Tailrace; RT1, Rock Island Tailrace near-BRZ.]

	Catch per 10 minutes			
	Northern pikeminnow		Smallmouth bass	
Reaches	Spring 2010	Summer 2010	Spring 2010	Summer 2010
PT2	0	0.011	0	0
PT1	0.127	0.064	0	0.010
PT0	0.080	0.008	0.015	0.016
PF0	0.075	0.035	0.155	0.100
PF1	0.018	0.021	0.036	0.087
PF2	0.032	0.033	0.010	0.028
PM3	0.030	0.034	0.020	0.015
WT2	0.030	0.005	0	0.002
WT1	0.046	0	0	0
WT0	0.074	0.025	0	0.020
WF0	0.060	0.010	0.110	0.060
WF1	0.027	0.017	0.013	0.033
WF2	0.006	0.019	0.010	0.007
WM3	0.091	0.098	0.001	0.005
RT2	0.043	0.055	0	0
RT1	0.036	0.052	0	0

Table 5. Predation indices estimated during the Burley and Poe sampling (Burley and Poe, 2009) in spring (May 27–June 12) and summer 2009 (August 3–20), and during Burley and Poe's 1993 study (Burley and Poe, 1994).

[Values presented for Burley and Poe's original study were estimated using a different density index (proportion of positive efforts) that was calculated from the values presented in their report and using different estimates of the areal extent of the proportion of the relevant reaches less than 3 meters in depth]

	Predation Index			
	Northern pikeminnow			
	Burley and Poe 2009		Burley and Poe 1993	
Reaches	Spring	Summer	Spring	Summer
PT1	31.0	0	71.0	109
PF1	0	0	2.38	0
PM3	0	0	0	0
WT1	7.57	0	56.5	120
WF1	2.13	0	17.1	0
WM3	9.42	0	0	0
RT1	0	0	11.6	1.29

Table 6. Predation indices and standard errors (in parentheses) estimated for northern pikeminnow and smallmouth bass captured during predator index sampling in spring (May 7–June 11) and summer 2009 (June 23–August 5), by reaches, Priest Rapids Project, Columbia River, Washington.

[Reach locations: PT1, Priest Rapids Tailrace; PT0, Priest Rapids Tailrace BRZ (Boat Restricted Zone); PF0, Priest Rapids Forebay BRZ; PF1, Priest Rapids Forebay; PM1, Priest Rapids Mid-Reservoir; WT1, Wanapum Tailrace; WT0, Wanapum Tailrace BRZ; WF0, Wanapum Forebay BRZ; WF1, Wanapum Forebay; WM1,Wanapum Mid-Reservoir; RT1,Rock Island Tailrace]

| | Predation Index | | | |
| | Northern pikeminnow | | Smallmouth bass | |
Reaches	Spring 2009	Summer 2009	Spring 2009	Summer 2009
PT1	1.754 (1.637)	0.565(0.565)	0	1.073 (1.073)
PT0	0	0	0	0
PF0	0	0	0.002 (0.002)	0.012 (0.007)
PF1	0	0	0.0.129 (0.129)	0
PM1	0	0	0.240 (0.240)	0.225 (0.225)
WT1	0	0	0	0
WT0	0	0	0	[a]
WF0	0	0	0	0
WF1	0	0	0	0
WM1	0	0	0	0.306 (0.306)
RT1	0	0	0	0

[a] - Not sampled

Table 7. Predation indices and standard errors (in parentheses) estimated for northern pikeminnow and smallmouth bass captured during predator index sampling in spring (May 2–June 9), and summer 2010 (June 27–August 11), by reaches, Priest Rapids Project, Columbia River, Washington.

[Reach locations: PT2, Priest Rapids Tailrace; PT1, Priest Rapids Tailrace near-BRZ; PT0, Priest Rapids Tailrace BRZ; PF0, Priest Rapids Forebay BRZ; PF1, Priest Rapids Forebay near-BRZ; PF2, Priest Rapids Forebay; PM3, Priest Rapids Mid-Reservoir; WT2, Wanapum Tailrace; WT1, Wanapum Tailrace near-BRZ; WT0, Wanapum Tailrace BRZ; WF0, Wanapum Forebay BRZ; WF1, Wanapum Forebay near-BRZ; WF2, Wanapum Forebay; WM3, Wanapum Mid-Reservoir; RT2, Rock Island Tailrace; RT1, Rock Island Tailrace near-BRZ.]

	Predation Index			
	Northern pikeminnow		Smallmouth bass	
Reaches	Spring 2010	Summer 2010	Spring 2010	Summer 2010
PT2	0	0	0	0
PT1	0.117 (0.051)	0	0	0
PT0	0	0	0	0.0
PF0	0	0	0.015 (0.015)	0.012 (0.012)
PF1	0	0	0.114 (0.114)	0.038 (0.025)
PF2	0	0	0	1.055 (0.776)
PM3	0.421(0.421)	0.196 (0.196)	5.940 (2.731)	1.760 (1.152)
WT2	1.018 (1.018)	0	0	0
WT1	0.157 (0.157)	0	0	0
WT0	0.015 (0.015)	0	0	0
WF0	0	0	0.090 (0.090)	0.109 (0.044)
WF1	0.011 (0.011)	0	0	0.113 (0.113)
WF2	0	0	0	0
WM3	1.918 (1.211)	0	0	0
RT2	0.274 (0.184)	0	0	0
RT1	0.011 (0.011)	0.016 (0.016)	0	0

www.ingramcontent.com/pod-product-compliance
Lightning Source LLC
Chambersburg PA
CBHW080433290526
45791CB00008BA/2477